T0352892

The Feel Good Home

Marion Hellweg

The *Feel Good* Home

A Practical Guide to Conscious Living

PRESTEL

Munich • New York • London

Curtain up
FOR YOUR HOME STAGE

'Emotions need space.' More and more people are taking this motto literally and setting up their personal retreat for their inner balance at home. We create spaces that are good for us, whether it's a music room, a mini library, a wellness bath or another kind of relaxation area. A safe haven where we can enjoy what is important to us is something that all age groups aspire to, including boomers, Gen X, Gen Z and Millennials. A feel-good home is our chosen 'place to be', especially at a time that does not seem very secure.

The topic of 'feeling good at home' is not just about beautiful furniture, atmospheric interior design and matching colours, however; above all it's about a perfect mixture of different factors that directly influence our wellbeing. It's crucial that all our senses are stimulated. Seeing, hearing, smelling, tasting and feeling – these are the classic five human senses, and together they serve as a base for our overall perception with which we experience impressions and stimuli from the environment, including everything within our four walls.

I hope that this book will help you to create your own 'feel-good home' – including everything that goes with it. You might just start by making yourself a cup of tea, listening to my playlist (see page 124) and relaxing as you read and flip through.

Live yourself happy!

"

We perceive our home with our five senses.

Contents

INTERVIEWS

Five

Senses

Waking up to the twittering of the birds, squinting into the early-morning sunlight, feeling the softness of our blanket – our five senses are in action from the second we wake to the moment we fall asleep.

Living creatures are dependent on their senses to get their bearings in the world, to distinguish friend from foe, to feed themselves and to survive. While some animals have additional, unusual super-senses, such as the ability to detect the Earth's magnetic field, human beings are limited to the classic five senses: hearing, sight, touch, taste and smell. Whether our nostrils are experiencing a new fragrance or our fingers are tickling a cat's fur, the process from original stimulus to the body's reaction is generally very similar for all the senses.

If a specific stimulus, such as a sudden noise or a new taste, hits the respective sensory organ, it is recorded by countless sensory cells and transmitted straight to the brain via nerve cells and pathways. The brain processes the stimulus, which then triggers a corresponding reaction.

Seeing

Keep your eyes open! It's not just in road-traffic situations that sight is of fundamental importance. The eyes will ideally detect hazards and obstacles in advance to allow the body to react accordingly. Yet the optic nerve also records other essential information. Is it a bright day or starry night? Is the mountain far away in the distance or does the incline start within a few metres? Where is the child playing in the garden and where has the dog managed to run off to? Our eyes also signal positive moments, however. The person we're talking to is smiling warmly at us. The sun is glinting magically through the treetops, and, thank goodness, the dog has found its way back on its own. Our sense of sight is the source of most of the information that all the senses ultimately send to the brain.

This is how it works: the cornea, which is basically the window of the eye, lets light rays in. The light falls through the pupil, which dilates or contracts, thereby determining the amount of light allowed in. The light is then focused by the lens and transmitted to the retina. As is also the case with cameras, the image received is upside down. It is the brain that rotates it 180 degrees to its correct position. There are around 130 million photoreceptor cells on the retina. The smaller proportion of these cells, the cones, is responsible for seeing colour. The rods make up the far greater proportion. They detect light and dark contrast. The cones are also responsible for sharp vision. As they are used less at twilight, the outlines and contours of what we're looking at become blurred. The less light there is, the more the rods have to work alone. At night, they are therefore totally on their own.

There are three different groups of cones, each of which perceive a specific colour gamut, namely red, blue and green. The brain pieces the information together, combines it with the information it has received about brightness, and consequently produces a coloured image. Having a defective cone results in colour blindness, such as red-green colour blindness.

All cats are grey at night – because colours only become visible when light comes into play. White light is made up of the so-called 'spectral colours' (red, orange, yellow, green, blue, indigo and violet) which we also see in rainbows. The world shines in full colour because every object and every living creature reflects some light rays, while absorbing some other light rays. Green plants, for example, absorb a lot of the red component of sunlight and primarily reflect the green component. The material that an object is composed of therefore determines which light rays are reflected and which are absorbed.

BLINK OF AN EYE

Are your eyes blue or brown, green or grey? The colour of your eyes is determined by the amount of melanin in the front layer of your eyes' irises. This creates the different colours. How much melanin exists in your own irises is primarily a question of heredity.

Right Of course, your speakers don't have to play music. There are also podcasts on every topic and for every taste.
Below left The infamous dripping water tap can certainly drive you round the bend.
Below right If you don't wish to annoy your neighbours or housemates, wear headphones when the music gets louder.

EAVESDROPPING

Noises are soundwaves. Hertz (Hz) is the unit that indicates vibrations per second. Humans perceive sound waves in a frequency range between 16 and 20,000 Hz; dogs can hear anything between 15 and 50,000 Hz; and bats discern noises between 20 and over 100,000 Hz.

Hearing

Pssst . . . did you hear that? Some sounds are so quiet you can hardly perceive them, like the proverbial pin dropping. Others, meanwhile, have us quickly block our ears. Incidentally, one of the loudest noises of all time was considered to be the bang that occurred when the Indonesian volcano Krakatoa erupted in 1883. Some noises make our hair stand on end, like the grating of a fork scraping against a smooth plate. Other sounds are wonderfully calming, such as the sound of the ocean's waves. Others again are so extraordinarily beautiful and moving that they bring tears to our eyes.

Our ears work 24/7. They're even in use while we're asleep, to alert us to potential dangers or alarms. In ancient times, this might have been something like the cracking of a tree branch which betrayed an approaching enemy or hungry predators. Today, it is more likely that we are disturbed by the noise of cars, lorries or planes.

The outer ear captures the sound waves – which are essentially fluctuating air pressure – like a funnel, before they make their way to the eardrum via the ear canal. They make the eardrum vibrate, and these vibrations are in turn sent from the ossicle to the cochlea, from where the signals are then transmitted straight to the brain.

In humans, the sense of hearing is more sensitive than the other four senses. The ear can detect up to 400,000 sounds, and can distinguish between ten entire octaves. Since we have two ears, it is no problem for our sense of hearing to pinpoint the direction the noises are coming from – a skill that is very helpful in more than just road-traffic scenarios.

Too much noise is unhealthy, which is why people working with loud machinery not only wear earmuffs, but are also required to take noise breaks. Even at home, we are often exposed to stressful noises. Incidentally, a constant noise, like that of a dripping tap, is often considered to cause more stress than the ever-changing banging and crashing from a construction site right outside our window – or a crying baby, an endless telephone chat or loud arguments in the next-door neighbour's house.

We should ensure calm surroundings at home wherever possible. After all, our hectic everyday lives are often loud and stressful enough. It is particularly important to create a tranquil zone in the bedroom to help you switch off and recharge in silence. Soundproof windows and insulating materials that absorb other noises, such as special wall panels, also help to maximise a sense of tranquillity in the home.

Feeling

Oh, how nice! Hugging the people you love, stroking a pet or just wrapping yourself in a cosy blanket – cuddling is just plain good for us. Touch is fundamentally important, particularly for the mind. Babies depend on physical contact for their healthy development, because the touch of the skin stimulates growth hormones and forms new connections in the brain. Yet the skin isn't just about soft, loving touches. It sounds out surfaces for important information. Is the tree trunk rough or smooth? Does the loudspeaker vibrate? Is the coffee cup hot or has it cooled? The skin explores all materials and surfaces, transmitting information about temperature, surface texture, pressure and solidity to the brain.

The skin is the largest sensory organ – it is indeed the largest organ in the human body. It holds the body together and surrounds it as a protective layer. It prevents the body from drying out and influences its temperature by producing sweat. On top of all that, it explores its surroundings and provides potentially life-saving information.

The skin is around one to two millimetres thick and consists of three layers. The topmost layer is the epidermis, beneath which is the dermis, which contains sweat glands and hair roots. The bottommost layer is called the subcutis, also known as the hypodermis, which contains fat cells, as well as blood vessels and nerves.

All three skin layers have receptors – sensory cells that detect external stimuli. But they're not all alike. Some receptors sit directly on the surface and can sense even the faintest of touches, while others sit deeper and react to things like pressure, pain, temperature, vibration . . . the countless different receptors in the skin provide information on whatever they touch.

Just as our skin doesn't feel the same in every part of the body, it similarly does not contain the same amount of sensory cells all over. The lips, for example, are particularly sensitive and can detect the slightest touch, whereas the back is normally not as responsive.

As human beings are the only living creatures to use their hands only to grip and hold things, our fingertips also contain a particularly large amount of sensory cells. After all, our hands are almost always in use and need to continuously send information to the brain. It's not just when reading Braille that they demonstrate their sensitivity; they also do so in completely everyday tasks – from checking the temperature of the first jets of water in our morning shower to lovingly patting the head of our sleeping pet.

Left Softer under your bum and legs, harder on the backrest – the body feels the seat with every point of contact. ***Below left*** A pet feels good on several levels – it's cuddly and soft, snuggly and warm, and exerts a pleasant pressure on your lap. ***Below right*** A fragrant bath is like a spa cure for all the senses.

CONSTANTLY NEW

It may be hard to believe, but our outermost layer of skin, the epidermis, completely renews itself every four weeks! To do so, it sheds a few grams of dead skin cells every day, while new cells are formed deeper down at its bottom layer and slowly migrate to the surface of the skin.

Smelling

Have a sniff! Doesn't this smell great? Pleasant smells instantly make us happy and bring a smile to our faces. Yet our noses don't just sniff out new perfumes, freshly baked biscuits, the scent of summer flowers, the fragrance of newly fallen rain or the aroma of our favourite dish. No, they also detect hazards, from gas leaks to rotting food or fire smoke. Our sense of smell identifies threats the eyes can't see and the ears can't hear. And that's not all: our noses also ensure that our meals veritably explode in our mouths – because, while the tongue can only distinguish five types of flavours, the nose can sniff out over 10,000 scent profiles. How amazing is it that our sense of smell is so closely tied in with our sense of taste, creating a complete, multi-faceted flavour experience!

Here's how smell works: the olfactory mucosa right at the top of our nasal cavities contain something between 10 and 30 million olfactory receptor cells, equipped with receptors capable of distinguishing over 350 different scents. Dogs, incidentally, have ten times as many olfactory receptor cells as humans. Humans, plants and many objects excrete odorant molecules. This fragrance information is sent via nerve pathways to the olfactory bulb in the brain, which is responsible for processing these signals. It combines and transmits them, making it effectively the control centre for processing smells.

Our sense of smell is almost fully developed before we even leave the womb. It is vital for our survival; after all, newborns follow their nose when searching for their mothers' milk. Their sense of smell also plays a role when bonding with their parents. Surprisingly, it's possible to further hone our olfactory abilities. If you were to work with fragrances, you would train this sense and sensitivity every day by specifically sniffing scents and classifying them.

The way to a person's heart may be through the stomach – but it is definitely also through the nose, and if you temporarily lose your sense of smell, your meals won't taste very good or indeed of anything. Conversely, you may feel that someone 'gets up your nose' because the odorant molecules humans excrete also contain information on their genetic makeup. And these are much more than idiomatic phrases. While two people are initially appraising each other visually and exchanging some first words, the brain has long checked whether or not there's any 'chemistry' between them. Research conducted on animals has shown that living creatures generally seek out partners whose genetic makeup information is the most different from their own. This means there's a good chance of producing strong, resilient offspring.

Left Pretty and decorative – sticks soak up the oils and release fragrance into the room.
Below left Fresh flowers are even prettier. Freesias, hyacinths and jasmine, for example, have an intense scent.
Below right An aroma diffuser can also help spread the desired scent in the room.

MEMORIES

In the first three years of your life you collect most of the information that is stored in your olfactory memory. Incidentally, memories are often associated with particular smells. If you detect the scent, the specific event or feeling is immediately brought back to mind.

Right Nothing beats a relaxed breakfast with an interesting book.
Below left To some people, coffee simply tastes too bitter, while others love exactly this intense aroma.
Below right If you cook fresh meals, chew thoroughly and concentrate on the food, you will train your tastebuds.

HAPPY EATERS

Sweet foods make you happy. This reaction of brain and body dates back to the times when a sweet taste meant you were eating food which contained carbohydrates and therefore energy. Survival was assured. Today, however, a box of chocolates can still guarantee pure happiness.

Tasting

Mmmm, yummy! Our tastebuds start to sing and dance whenever culinary delights find their way into our mouths. Favourite meals instantly put us in a good mood, comfort food tastes like a sense of security and solace, while new flavours and unfamiliar ingredients and dishes create completely new experiences and moments of indulgence. Our sense of taste isn't just about enjoying delicious treats, however; it also recognise things unfit for consumption. Extreme bitterness, for example, immediately repulses us, because humans used to be dependent on their sense of taste as a means of distinguishing between toxic and non-toxic foods – and many poisonous plants have a bitter taste.

Your sense of taste gets to work as soon as the first spoonful of vegetable soup lands in your mouth. Its most important tool is your tongue, whose surface contains the papillae – tiny mounds that are partially also visible to the naked eye. It's the papillae that absorb the flavouring substances, and inside these are the tastebuds, of which every human has thousands. Each tastebud in turn has up to 100 taste receptor cells, which collect the important information and transmit it to the cerebral cortex, where it is combined with information from the sense of smell. This creates a richly layered impression of the vegetable

soup's composition, and this is of course also where you determine whether the dish is to your liking or not.

While humans are able to detect countless different types of smells, they can only distinguish between five types of tastes: sweet and salty, bitter and sour. The fifth is called umami, or savouriness, which denotes a spicy flavour found in high-protein foods like cheese or meat. Each type of taste stimulates the receptor cells differently, and is transmitted to the brain through the nerves.

The number of tastebuds decreases as we age. While a young person still has around 9,000, older people only have about half as many. In other words, our sense of taste dwindles over the years. Yet what we eat also affects our personal perception of taste. If you mostly eat freshly prepared food, you will have a much better sense of taste than someone who eats primarily flavour-enhanced ready-made meals.

Arch

itecture

A house is much more than just a roof over your head. It's a personal space where you can shut the door on the outside world and unwind. It's also a home, a focal point that brings friends and family together.

Whether Stone Age cave or futuristic new edifice, the number one priority for any form of housing has always been to provide shelter, followed closely by the need to make this sanctuary as attractive as possible. Obviously there were limited ways to do this in caves, but through the millennia, people began placing increasing importance both on interior and exterior design. In fact, it's not really possible to separate the building shell from the life that goes on within it, because architecture also plays a major role in the notion of feeling good at home.

Are there enough rooms and how are they laid out? Does the floor plan meet the needs of the people who live there? How much light floods the rooms, and at what time of day? Will the building materials create the best possible vibe in the home? Architecture needs to answer all these and similar questions.

Buildings FOR LIFE

An industrial-chic loft; a romantic country cottage with a potager garden; a renovated terraced house; a tiny mobile home; or a character-filled flat in an old building – what's your architectural style of choice?

LIVEABLE CITIES

A key aim of modern town planning is to create pleasant neighbourhoods where people can live, work and spend their leisure time – an eclectic mix of cultural and social life with sustainability and climate protection writ large.

> " Architecture creates new individual living spaces.

Top right Farmhouses with thatched roofs are particularly common in northern Europe.
Above left Apartments in former warehouses or factory buildings exude a cool industrial charm.
Above right Curved balcony lines elegantly break up the rigidity and edges of this façade.
Right It couldn't be any more minimalist – a tiny house hidden inside plain concrete walls.

From Past
TO PRESENT

As you walk through any city's streets, every façade has a different story to tell. There's no better evidence of the passage of time than the buildings that were erected in different eras. Churches, temples and other official buildings are among the best-preserved examples.

The edifices built in centuries past were all shaped by different styles and periods in art and architecture. Thus, Antiquity was followed by the Romanesque period, which lasted from around 1000 to 1250. Solid walls, box-like shapes and small windows with round arches were designed to make religious buildings and castles look rather forbidding, almost impenetrable. By contrast, the structures of the Gothic period were much more delicate. From 1140 to 1520, people built soaring churches, monasteries, castles and town halls, all heavily adorned with pointed arches, ornamental gables, turrets and stained-glass windows – Notre-Dame Cathedral in Paris is one of the most famous examples. The Renaissance, in the fifteenth and sixteenth centuries, meanwhile, tried to keep things nicely in balance. Symmetry and harmony played key roles. Domes and round arches, arcades and columns featured on both secular and religious buildings, such as St Peter's Basilica in Rome. During the Baroque period, from the early seventeenth century to the 1750s, opulence ruled supreme – more was definitely more. Aristocracy and clergy alike underlined their status by commissioning magnificent buildings, featuring sweeping designs, marble, gold, sculptures and stucco. The Palace of Versailles is a fine example. The Neoclassical period, from the mid-eighteenth to the mid-nineteenth centuries, acted as a countermovement of sorts, using clean lines, hulking, angular shapes and symmetrical columns to replace all the frivolity. The White House in Washington D.C. exemplifies this style. Historicism, which dominated from the mid- to the late nineteenth century, copied the styles of previous epochs, primarily to beautify façades.

Architectural preferences changed at a faster rate in the twentieth century, with different styles following each other in quick succession. It all began with Art Nouveau. Until 1920, nature served as the template for sweeping – and often also asymmetrical – shapes and decorative floral elements.

Left Seen from the right point of view, a successful architectural element becomes a work of art – just like this staircase.

From 1920 to 1940, Art Deco picked up on the idea of using tendrils, petals and leaves, contrasting them with rigid geometry. Construction materials such as glass and metal further enhanced this flamboyance. The Chrysler Building in New York is a world-famous example. The minimalist Bauhaus style, named after the eponymous German school of art, design and architecture, emerged at the same time. Its followers reduced design to the bare essentials, to clean lines and simple forms. The Bauhaus look ties in closely with that of Modernity. From 1910 to 1960, architecture was all about no-frills objectivity, using clean materials such as glass, steel and concrete. 'Form follows function' and 'less is more' were guiding principles of that particular epoch, which was also known as mid-century modern in the USA. The subsequent Postmodernist style liberated itself from this rigidity. Once again, façades became more elaborate and striking, drawing on elements from various epochs of the past.

Today, buildings have to factor in not only functionality, but also sustainability. Eco-friendly construction materials and energy-efficient concepts are the main focus of many designs, and this pragmatism is also reflected in the forms. You'll be hard pushed to find opulent adornments, protrusions, bays, turrets, recesses or intertwined elements. Simple structures are the fashion of the day, and they're also cheaper to manufacture and more energy-efficient. This practical aspect doesn't diminish their visual appeal or homeliness in any way, however. Floor-to-ceiling windows and large glass façades admit abundant daylight, while also bringing the surrounding nature inside, and delicate, filigree elements further neutralise the rigidity and heaviness of the bulky, solid shapes of such structures.

Above This house seems to be cast as one, with roof and walls apparently merging. The wide window front admits the green outdoors into the living space.
Far left Natural stone, cement, wood – materials that used to be papered or painted over in the past – today add a special charm to a home.
Left Wooden cladding guides the eye to the ceiling and the open roof space, underlining the shape of the room.

Natural materials are another way of achieving an attractive overall look. As an added bonus, they create a healthy indoor climate and a cosy ambience. Wood, for example, is not just a sustainable construction material – homes made from timbers such as spruce and larch are also extremely comfortable to live in. Those seeking a modern look can clad external or internal walls with wood panelling instead of slats or boards. Another material that had long sunk into oblivion but is now making a comeback is adobe. Made from earth and organic materials, adobe can be recycled over and over. It is also efficient at storing heat and creates a pleasant indoor climate by filtering and binding toxins from the air and regulating humidity. Even concrete has unexpected benefits – it can be cast into any conceivable shape and made from regional materials; it stores heat and is extremely durable; and it also goes superbly with today's look.

Left *Metal, wood, stone, glass and water – a mix of materials links the two parts of the building, which date from different decades, into an exciting unified whole.*
Top *The glazed front not only emphasises the shape of the gable, it also allows light and nature into the interior of the building.*
Right *By opening up this modern living space to the floor above, an airy, spacious atmosphere is created, and the gallery affords great views down to the lower floor.*

Right Let's all cuddle up! Is the living area spacious enough for all family members to find a comfortable place?
Below left Hang on in there! A climbing wall in the children's room, a racetrack in the hall, a swing in the living room: children should be able to move freely.
Below right The great outdoors – happiness is an outside space. If there isn't one, let's just go to the park.

YOURS & MINE

To ensure people can live together harmoniously, it is important to define different areas. Where can kids scatter all their toys, for example? Which corners are adults-only? Separate areas allow you to create tidy spaces, and you will also spare yourself many an argument.

HAPPY
Families

With everyone living under one roof, there's always plenty of action in a family household. Each person has their own agenda and plans, their own needs and wants, their own tasks and duties – both at home and in the outside world. What does 'home' mean to the whole family? It's a port of call for everyone; the roof under which all the bustle of life happens, where everyone comes together, but also where each person has their own living space to rest and unwind.

That's a hefty load of requirements for a home, but a spacious flat in an old building can accommodate them just as easily as a newly built home tailored specifically to the needs of its inhabitants. Do you live in a small flat or in a house with a less-than-ideal floor plan? It might be worth thinking about a major makeover to transform it into a feel-good space for the whole family.

Family life generally revolves around one particular piece of furniture – the table. It's where all the family members gather, where they eat, celebrate, study, play and have discussions. It's a place to do homework, and it can also act as a home office. Naturally, this table also demands suitable, homely surroundings. So a spacious dining area or a kitchen large enough to accommodate this pivotal piece of furniture, together with lots of chairs or benches around it, will be the heart of any family home.

Sufficient space for a large, comfy sofa is, however, almost as important. Such a lounge area is perfect for movie nights or cuddle sessions, for romping around or for a relaxed evening without the kids.

In addition to these common areas, it is fundamentally important to have places to which each family member can retreat – a room or at least a corner where both children and adults can do their own thing without being disturbed; a place where they can enjoy peace and quiet, but which they can also style according to their own personal tastes.

An open-plan design lets in light and air, and is particularly perfect for families with younger children. No matter what you're doing, you'll always be able to keep an eye on the little ones. Generally, kids absolutely love being in the middle of everything that's going on around them. As they get older, however, they usually like to retreat to their own private space.

Another important aspect when you share your home with children is that they will need a room or other space for games. If the house has a garden of sorts – perfect. A large balcony or terrace are equally good, but even if there is no such outdoor space, a large living room or a long corridor will work equally well for acrobatics and other fun.

Living ALONE OR AS A COUPLE

Whether you are in a home of your own for the first time or downsizing as empty-nesters, living in student digs or a second home or designing a large dream home for two, the living spaces for singles and couples will vary as much as the people themselves. It's equally difficult to generalise what requirements each home needs to meet, but one thing is for sure – no matter whether you live alone or as a couple, you will probably be much more flexible in terms of the room layout and the architecture than a family with kids. A spacious loft is perfect for singles, and also for couples if there are spaces to retreat to. A tiny attic flat, on the other hand, is great for anyone who doesn't need much space but loves the panoramic city views.

If your home is mainly a place to relax, then you won't need much floor space and will be happy in a smaller flat. If you are also working from home, then a dedicated office space is a must. This could be just a separate little screened-off corner in the living room, although an actual study where you can shut the door behind you once you've finished for the day is preferable. If you have guests staying overnight, you may want to place a sofa bed in your home office. Do you enjoy cooking or is the kitchen used mostly as a home for the coffee machine? If you like to don your chef's hat and apron, you're going to need space around the stove and the fridge. Perhaps a large kitchen diner would be a good solution, with a table around which family and friends can gather.

More and more people fancy the idea of living in a tiny home. Living space is become increasingly scarce and expensive, particularly in the big cities, so minimising the floor space is a necessity. Some people, however, just want to completely declutter and concentrate on the bare essentials. There again, a tiny home may provide an excellent alternative.

Feeling good at home is not about size. If the floor plan works and everything that's important fits in, it is entirely possible to live well in small confines. It's just a matter of utilising the space to best effect. For example, the stairs to the loft bedroom could be used for storage, and the table can double as a social space and as an office desk. Creativity is key here to making it work.

Left A kitchen diner can be the perfect solution for one or two people. After all, it offers space for entertaining guests, working and lots of life.
Below left Even a small room can accommodate lots – from the kitchen workspace and dining area via work station and storage space to lounge corner.
Below right Many couples also need a quiet space to retreat to.

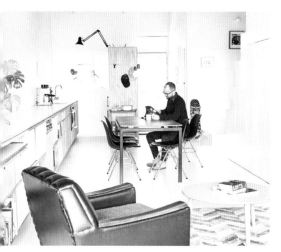

SPACE MIRACLE

You want to know all about living in a small space? You'll find lots of information here:
• Marion Hellweg, *Tiny Homes* (Prestel, 2021)
• tinyecohomesuk.com
• thetinyhousing.co
• thetinylife.com

6 Gables,
ONE ROOF

Jennifer Bonner
Haus Gables

When it comes to architecture, Jennifer Bonner likes breaking new ground. Why not layer a building like a sandwich? Or design a house from the roof down? She shares her creative approaches with students at the Harvard University Graduate School of Design as an associate professor. And in 2009 she founded MALL, a creative agency that tackles new projects in totally unconventional ways. For more information, visit jenniferbonner.com.

Jennifer, even as a child, you were influenced by your father's architecture software, and you constructed your first building as a 22-year-old university student. How did your career progress from there?

After college, I spent a few years working in London – at Forster + Partners and at David Chipperfield Architects. I then returned to the US and completed my studies at the Harvard University Graduate School of Design, where, some years later, I now teach as an associate professor. Originally, I wanted to work at an architectural firm for a few years after completing my studies and before becoming self-employed but, during the 2009 recession, jobs were extremely hard to come by. So, out of sheer necessity, I founded my own firm and did teaching on the side – and that's exactly what I still do today.

Your company is called MALL. What's the story behind this?

I chose the name because it is as flexible as the ideas and projects behind it. MALL stands for 'Mass Architectural Loopty Loops', but it could just as easily mean 'Miniature Angles and Little Lines', or even 'Maximum Arches with Limited Liability'. We're not bound to any specific meaning when it comes to our company name, and, similarly, we do not focus on one specific direction in our projects. In 2014, for example, I developed a project I named 'Domestic Hats', which involved studying and typologising all kinds of different roof shapes. On my computer, I devised sixteen mass models of roofs, that is, architectural models that only show the base form of each one. These models were then blown up into oversized versions and went on display as part of an exhibition in Atlanta. My fascination with roofs and roof shapes was also the driving force behind Haus Gables.

__Left__ A lot of house in a small area – the extravagant roof shape makes the narrow rooms appear very airy.

Left *Some high up, some low down, some large, some small – the windows appear as if they have been randomly placed.*
Right *CLT-panel cladding supports the effect of the architectural forms.*

utility room and bathroom from the rest of the floor. When seen from the street, the building makes you stop and stare, because the classic gables have been replaced with a flamboyant, asymmetrical shape. It is also unusually narrow, which makes it a great idea for architecture in densely built-up areas.

What exactly is this CLT?

CLT stands for cross-laminated timber. Several single-layer slats are glued together crossways to create an amazing construction material. CLT is sustainable, has interesting textures and is a real game-changer for architecture. I would never have been able to achieve this sophisticated geometry with conventional beams. CLT is able to perform structural gymnastics. The panels can be used to construct solid wall structures or for indoor cladding.

What do you love most about Haus Gables?

I love the fact that the house looks like one of my 'Domestic Hats' models. I love the fact that architecture can be a representational project before actually being constructed. So, in fact, I love the entire process from exhibition piece to finished home. And I also love how unusual the building looks as you approach it from the street – a real eye-catcher.

Haus Gables doesn't just exist as a mass model, but is an actual residential building in Atlanta, Georgia. Would you like to tell us a bit more about that?

Haus Gables was created from one of those models. I was wondering what it would be like to design a building entirely geared around the roof if the building's floor plan followed the roof layout. Unfortunately, I didn't have any clients wanting to commission just such a building, and so my husband and I decided to make this our own personal project – a family home for my husband, our daughter and me; a building where the roof sets the tone and decides the outcome, constructed from my favourite material, CLT (which stands for cross-laminated timber) – my absolute dream assignment.

And what does this family dream house look like now that it's finished?

Haus Gables combines six gables that collectively form a roof. They create the space beneath them through peaks and troughs, determining the building's floor plan. They define the size and shape of the rooms, the hallways and the gallery. Many areas flow into each other. What I find important are the lines of sight and interesting angles, of which there are 55 in total. To preserve them, I minimised the number of doors used; on the upper level, there's a door that can be used to partition the bedroom from the bathroom, and on the ground floor, two sliding doors separate the

"

Haus Gables represents new form and materials.

Sense

# of Space

Four walls, a ceiling, a floor, a door and a window or two or three. Do you think the room is finished? Not quite. A comfortable sense of space is all about perceived size.

Whether you're on a large square outside the train station or in a cramped guest bathroom, between rows of supermarket shelves or in a narrow office corridor – wherever you go in the built environment you are surrounded by spatial boundaries. Whether these are vast and expansive, or small and compact, the sense of space affects your wellbeing.

Being able to cast your gaze around and relish the openness without feeling hemmed in is important for enjoying a sense of freedom and being able to breathe when you're at home. You also want to feel safe and protected. It's a major task for architecture to create a good sense of space, and although it needs to deal with limitations, there are a few tricks you can use to change spatial perceptions for optimum look and feel. After all, you don't want your feel-good home to be let down by a poor room layout.

LET IT ALL *Flow*

Everything – from your outlook on life and your breathing to your thoughts – flows better in spaces that feel open and airy. This isn't true just for big houses; it works just as well in small flats and even tiny homes.

FLYING HIGH!

High ceilings can preserve a sense of space even if the floor plan only allows for small and narrow rooms. Try to open out the ceiling as much as possible. Ceilings in older buildings have often been lowered – it's definitely worth reversing this to get rid of any panelling and open out the rooms vertically to maximise the overall sense of space.

Left *This hallway has gained a lot from being opened up to the roof and given whitewashed wood panelling.*
Top right *In an old building, double doors automatically create a great feeling of spaciousness.*
Right *If you can afford to open out the view from one room to the next, you'll convey a sense of generous space.*
Far right *Colours can enhance the general perception of roominess.*

"

Take a deep breath and you'll start to feel well.

HEIGHT, WIDTH AND *Depth*

A long and stressful day at the office, heavy traffic and lousy weather – it's just one of those occasions when your home becomes your ultimate refuge. It's where you shake the rain out of your hair, put on your warm slippers and surround yourself with your loved ones and prized possessions. It's the place to shed any stress, pressure and anxiety and take a deep breath, and this will of course be much more effective if you are comfortable overall in your own four walls. The sense of space, the feeling you get from the rooms and hallways, is an important factor here. Are they large and open or small and narrow? Are they light-filled or rather darker and more cramped? Sometimes, on a day when everything seems to be going wrong, you just want to shut yourself away at home and block out the world. In such a situation, a cosy den may be perfect. In general, however, a feel-good home means a home where you can breathe. It may sound odd, but a sense of space will see your shoulders relax, your breathing get deeper and

your mind slow down. There is room for your thoughts and gaze to wander, without becoming obstructed or hemmed in. After all, your home is a place to unwind, to take a breather and recharge your batteries. And the bigger the space, the easier it will be to experience a feeling of relaxation.

Sometimes you can get lucky. If you live in an older building you are likely to have high ceilings and long corridors. There may even be floor-to-ceiling doors that open between rooms, and windows that let in lots of natural light. It is particularly common for old townhouses to have several rooms located one behind the other, so that, once their doors are open, you can see from one end of the house to the other. They create an illusion that there is a lot of space even if the rooms themselves are not that large. High ceilings, which were generally more prevalent in decades past, also create a sense of airiness. But you can achieve the right vibe even in small flats and homes.

The trick is to open out the spaces to generate a feeling of vastness. So, if you can, knock down any obstructive walls or create large gaps. Even broadening a doorway or enlarging windows can really change things. Obviously these measures won't be feasible everywhere – especially in rented properties. So what tricks

Left Open the door, please. This way, your gaze does not stay within the room but can wander around freely.

can you use to create a feeling of spaciousness when the basic structure of the flat or house isn't exactly conducive to this?

Simply leave the doors wide open where possible, or, ideally, take them out altogether. When you can see from one room through to the next, everything seems more open and less restricted. Plus, you can create some exciting new perspectives. Placing an eye-catching object, such as an attractive piece of furniture or a picture, at the end of such interconnected rooms will inevitably draw a visitor's attention into the distance. This trick allows you to invent exciting new angles and perspectives without structurally changing the rooms at all.

The deliberate use of colour is something that never fails to change a room's look and feel, and it is equally simple. If you keep your walls, ceilings and floors in light colours, you will make a space automatically look bigger. And this effect is further enhanced when your furnishings are also kept on the lighter end of the colour spectrum.

When it comes to floors, however, it's not just colour that influences the sense of space. In the case of floorboards and parquet flooring, the direction in which they are laid is also a factor. Floorboards laid horizontally, such as on thresholds, act like a brake to a visitor's gaze, whereas floors laid consistently in the same direction throughout the entire home or level, following the same 'vertical' or 'lengthways' direction as your line of vision when you step through the door, will make your home seem significantly larger.

Textiles can also influence your perception. Thick curtains either side of the window restrict the view of the outside world. Light, airy, unobtrusive drapes or blinds, on the other hand, will allow more of the great outdoors in, creating a feeling of space.

Above White walls, a white floor, white furniture plus pale wood for more lightness – the colour concept makes this living room appear much larger than it actually is.

Far left The blue colour scheme around the bed transforms this room into a cosy spot.

Left You can subdivide an apartment into different areas with a carpet, counter and wooden cube without sacrificing space.

ROOM
Partitions

If you live in a loft, you'll love the feeling of expansiveness. Everything is open and spread over a large area, creating a great sense of space. Sometimes, however, this can feel overwhelming, to the point that you end up wanting some cosy corners. Open-plan living and dining areas can also occasionally do with some partitioning. When there's not enough privacy, when you don't always want the corner that you use as your home office or the play area to be visible, then you need practical solutions. After all, it's probably not a bad idea to move those stacks of folders out of sight once you've knocked off for the day, and ditto for toy cars and building blocks. The need for separate spaces exists no matter how big or small a home. This kind of partitioning and subdividing does not have to disrupt the sense of space, especially if it's done in a flexible way that does not cause any visual obstruction.

Simply move your furniture to visually separate the home office, lounge or play corner from the rest of the room; use your furniture to make partitioners. A couch in the middle of the room can act as a boundary between the cosy sitting area and the rest of the hustle and bustle. A sideboard or wide chest of drawers makes for a clearer distinction,

with the added bonus of storage space. A tall shelving unit delimiting two areas provides even more storage space and is also a clearer partition. If this piece of furniture has an enclosed rear side, it will look bulkier and more imposing than one with open compartments all the way down. You can fill the open version as much or as little as you wish to create either more privacy or airiness. Random bits and bobs can be stowed away in boxes to keep everything neat and tidy.

Why should curtains only ever be used to block out daylight or inquisitive looks? They work equally well as delicate partitions to separate a corner from the rest of the room. Their biggest plus point is that you use them only when needed. Otherwise you can keep them open to maintain a sense of spaciousness.

Folding screens and other partitions offer similar flexibility. They can be put up in no time when you want to take an afternoon siesta on the sofa or hide a messy play corner from guests. Some are so stylish that you can casually lean them against the wall as decorative elements when they are not needed.

The use of different levels also helps to separate areas from each other. While bunk beds are the most obvious version, a simple platform can equally provide sufficient space for a bed as well as ample storage room underneath, for example. Sofas and desks can also be raised to the next level.

Left This screen made of Viennese mesh looks nice and airy. During the day it's moved aside, while in the evening it ensures a good night's sleep.
Below left Curtains are the least complicated way to quickly create new rooms – and then to simply make them disappear again.
Below right If you decide to create separate corners and niches with shelves, you should ensure a wide access so that the space does not feel too narrow.

ROOM-IN-ROOM

One way of visually partitioning areas without actually putting up a physical barrier is to create a 'room within a room', as shown on p.44. Give walls and floors a different colour to the rest of the space or cover them so they look totally different, without encroaching on space.

OPEN *Space*

Kathrin Strauß
raumplus

From sliding doors to built-in cupboards, raumplus designs and produces furnishing systems for customers all over the world. With its smart wardrobes and accessible living solutions, the company is also well placed when it comes to innovations and research. Art Director and Head of Marketing, Kathrin knows all about using clever design to create a pleasant sense of space.
raumplus.com

How do you create a good sense of space?
For me, a good sense of space is created through the interplay of its elements – colours, shapes and functions – in other words, thinking about the purpose the space is supposed to fulfil. A large auditorium can create a good sense of space through light and ventilation, while a small restaurant can do so by having the right furnishings and an inviting aroma, and an office can use its acoustics and the feel of its work areas. What I always consider important are lighting, indoor air temperature, cohesive proportions and a certain unique individual aesthetic.

And how do you achieve that in your own four walls?
I try to achieve that by making the furnishings vibrant and dynamic, among other things. As a family, we want to feel comfortable, and colours, shapes and functions play a key role here, because we live with the furnishings and in the spaces. I always try to create a certain room aesthetic, with stylish but functional lighting and a good interplay between classics and modern elements.

'Raum' means both 'space' and 'room' in German, so Raumplus basically has in its name a sense of space – or more space. How do you create this extra space?
We create space by using partition systems and sliding doors. We custom-make the suitable elements in order to create a room within a room. It might be a classic office situation, or you may need to separate living and dining areas, or you want a dressing room within your existing bedroom or many other things. And this works also if you don't have a large loft flat. Our space solutions are always tailored to clients' wishes and requirements wherever technically possible.

Left *A harmony of form, colour and function will create a good sense of space.*

made wardrobe with an angled door, a lockable home office with small desk and ample storage space for all the files and computer accessories, or any number of other possibilities. This way, even less appealing dark corners can be used effectively and attractively.

What are the advantages of built-in cupboards – and in particular in terms of a sense of space?

Built-in cupboards do not actually stand in the room like other pieces of furniture; they're a fixed element of the very same room. This way, a wall and cupboard could form one cohesive front, creating a look of uniformity and harmony. As an added bonus, they also keep attention away from the sometimes not quite so attractive elements on the side. Built-in cupboards are always custom-made, so they utilise all the available space, with not a square inch going to waste. Additionally, they can be used in challenging areas such as alcoves, under sloping roofs or in the often wasted space under staircases. There are suitable profile systems, panels and surfaces for every possible situation. This keeps the aesthetics cohesive, while also creating a uniform, harmonious sense of space with a more open, expansive feel.

What's the best way to partition a room without negatively affecting the overall sense of space?

Each design is of course unique. Light definitely plays a major role. If the sliding doors and partitions are transparent, for example because they feature large glass panes, they will clearly separate the spaces, while still ensuring they look large and light-flooded. In my view, there certainly should never be any rupture in the spatial design causing partitions and room dividers to look like foreign bodies and harsh visual boundaries. The use of bright, lightweight panes should always enhance the existing space. If the partitions allow you to see into the next space, you can even pick up on existing colours and textures here to create a cohesive overall sense of space.

When it comes to preserving a sense of space, it's important to use the existing area as effectively as possible, for example to keep things neat and orderly. How does this work in alcoves and sloping spaces?

For alcoves, there are perfect storage solutions that can be designed as striking eye-catchers or unobtrusive elements, depending on what the client prefers. Spaces under sloping roofs can certainly also be utilised and fully integrated into the room. They may be in the form of a custom-

Each room needs an aesthetic of its own.

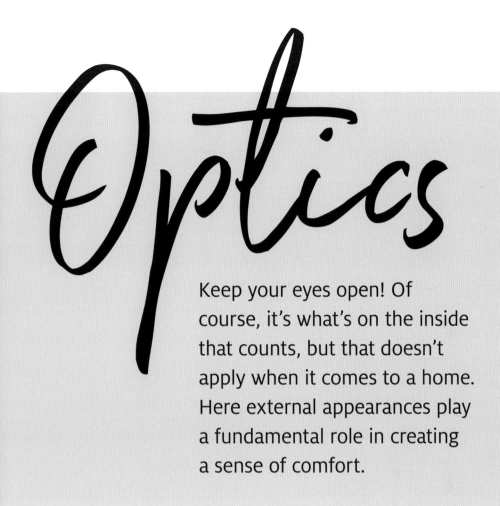

Optics

Keep your eyes open! Of course, it's what's on the inside that counts, but that doesn't apply when it comes to a home. Here external appearances play a fundamental role in creating a sense of comfort.

The word 'optics' comes from the Greek language and denotes anything to do with vision, sight or light. From a physics point of view, optics are all about light – how it diffuses, how it fragments and how it is reflected. That, of course, also involves colours – which we wouldn't even be able to see without light. Any visual information is rapidly transmitted from the eyes to the brain, triggering all kinds of reactions, for example a feeling of relaxed ease.

So there is no question that optics – or, more precisely, colours – are among the most important tools when it comes to transforming a house into a feel-good home, into a home that exudes a sense of comfort as soon as you open the door. Using colours is therefore a must – but which shades and hues are best suited for creating a comfortable ambience?

Colourful EFFECTS

What will you go for, wild romanticism or understated naturalism, fancy graphics or simple minimalism? When it comes to walls, the options are wide-ranging – that's as long as the overall effect is homely.

LET'S PLAY!

Your favourite colours are green and pink? That's excellent. Now let's play around with the wildest combinations – from olive and dusky rose to reed green and blush pink. Use a moodboard to try out pattern combinations and colour shades. Not only is this fun to do, but it will also give you a good idea of what best matches your personal preferences and your home's interior design.

Left Colourful can also mean delicate and rather gentle. This wall is painted in a fairly light shade and, together with a decoration of natural fibres, forms a calm, relaxed background for furniture that itself is also tranquil. This effect is further enhanced if the floor is in a similar shade to the walls. With this colour scheme, the room exudes a natural, relaxing cosiness.

> Simply experiment with
> colours and patterns!

Walls
IN FOCUS

Walls are perfect for playing with colours, patterns and other decorative elements to set different moods and create your very own ambience of wellbeing. After all, they are quietly in the background, allowing furniture and accessories to play the lead role. Walls provide the stage on which all of life happens, where the interior and, in particular, the people who live inside them take the spotlight. Yet they're much more than merely a basic architectural need. Quite the contrary. Walls give a home its framework. They surround the inhabitants like a protective shell. They create niches and cosy spaces, or open out to provide a sense of generous spaciousness. Their imposing size can also act as perfect, large canvases for your personalised styling.

In other words, your own four walls play an important role in feel-good optics, so be sure to give them your full attention. After all, walls that have been styled in the optimal way can look absolutely stunning. It's not just about exciting eye-catchers, however.

Left In combination with white and natural wood, a light shade of grey transform the room into an oasis of tranquillity.

Above all, designing your walls is about finding the right optics to create a comfortable and welcoming home.

A lick of paint

Painting walls in a different colour is the easiest way to change that room's vibe, and such a change can sometimes be drastic. A bucket of paint can seamlessly transform a dark, cramped room into a homely, open space – at least visually.

However, before you start getting out your paintbrushes, there are a few things to think about. What size and shape is the room you're about to attack? Pale colours can make small rooms look much brighter, and will certainly give them the feeling of having grown by a few square metres. They also add a sense of space to dark corners and recesses, making them appear almost light-filled. Oversized rooms or rooms with particularly high ceilings can, on the other hand, be rendered cosier and more intimate with darker shades. Small rooms can of course also be painted in dark colours for greater impact. A guest bathroom with dark green or anthracite walls, for example, is bound to surprise – and gain a few fans with its look. A tip for low ceilings or cramped rooms is to not paint all the way up to the ceiling;

Far left *Less is more? That's not the case, however, if different shades of colour family are as skilfully employed as here.*
Left *Floor, bench and walls are in perfect harmony.*
Bottom *A white accent counterpart cleverly makes darker shades glow.*

allow for a strip in the same colour as the ceiling. This visually extends the room. Doors and skirting boards can be painted in the same colour as the wall – it will make everything look more spacious.

Light is another important point. The larger the window and the more daylight that floods the room, the more effective darker or more intense colours become. If you're unsure, paint a wall at right angles to a window in the darker colour and choose lighter shades for other walls that are not as exposed to daylight. Internal corridors and bathrooms can only be brightened up with artificial lighting. Colours look completely different here compared to how they appear in natural light.

How much colour should you use? If you're painting only one wall, make it a striking feature that attracts everyone's attention to that side of the room. It's the perfect option if, for example, you've got your favourite picture hanging there as a centrepiece. You can also use this approach to draw focus to architectural details or a favourite furniture item. Incidentally, feature walls work best when they are one consistent area, not broken up with openings. Another worthwhile tip is that painting two opposite walls in the same intense colour will make the space look narrower. While this may be beneficial for wide rooms, it can leave narrow spaces feeling like a constricting tube or tunnel.

Left This gentle cloudscape has an amazingly relaxing effect, being excitingly attractive at the same time.
Below This extravagant wall is the main eye-catcher in the home. Instead of competitors, it demands a restrained background design.
Right As in the other examples, this wallpaper brings an unexpected depth to the room. Both pattern and colour are perfect choices for a bedroom.

Redecorating the walls

What will you choose – gentle dabs of colour, captivating patterns or large-scale illustrations? There is a clear trend towards wallpaper, the stylish alternative to paint. While it was considered stuffy and boringly suburban for decades, people have long since returned to papering the walls of kids' rooms, bedrooms, living rooms, corridors and even kitchens and bathrooms.

There's wallpaper to suit every style and taste, from floral to expressive patterns. The rule of thumb to bear in mind for a feel-good home is that the more exciting the wallpaper, the more low-key the furnishing needs to be; otherwise the space will quickly become overwhelming with too much visual detail. Simple graphic patterns in muted colours work almost anywhere. Landscapes, on the other hand, whether as photographic images or illustrations, will dominate the space and are ideally only used as a single piece on one wall. Anyone wanting to test out this form of wall

decoration should initially just use one, two or three sheets to highlight a particular area.

It's all in the frame

The best and most personal way of enhancing your walls is through pictures. It doesn't have to be a whole gallery wall; your favourite works of art can be enough to accentuate a space as individual pieces.

Whether holiday photos or children's drawings, oil paintings or art prints – if you like them, you can hang them on the wall. To prevent any visual chaos, there needs to be a thread that links the individual pieces. This could be the type, material or colour of the frames, or it could be the dominant colour schemes in the pictures. A collection of black-and-white pieces of artwork, for instance, always looks harmonious, even if it's a mixture of pencil drawings, photographs and acrylic images. Holiday or family snapshots can have their own commonalities just as easily as typographic pieces or different artworks that revolve around the same or a related theme.

Above A statement wall in dark blue or grey allows the colours of the works of art to stand out.
Far left Of course, instead of hanging them, you can also lean your pictures against the wall. Here the panelling serves as a unified picture ledge.
Left A small gallery on the sideboard or shelf can be added to and replaced as you like, and artistically rearranged over and over again.

One kitchen, three very different colour schemes:
Right *Cream looks bright and friendly, and the blue stripe hints at a window with views of the sky.*
Below left *Soft shades of eucalyptus paired with light olive hues and a light blue band – this kitchen is full of freshness and warmth.*
Below right *A dainty blush colour makes for a beautiful modern alternative to white.*

MORE THAN ONE – COMBINING COLOURS

What happens if you simply cannot decide which colour to choose? Just pick two, or even three, instead. Mixing different shades and hues also works magnificently on walls. You can, for example, just as easily paint each wall in a room in completely different colours as you can paint them in similar shades. Combining different colours on the same wall is another good option. Separating them horizontally has a similar effect to half-wall-height wood panelling, while vertical separation with different colours demarcates different living areas and uses.

COLOURFUL
Effects

Below *White walls create a clean look.* **Bottom** *The clever combination of colours creates a cosy, modern ambience.*

Colours influence the general ambience in all kinds of ways. If you know how they work, you can choose the right shades for your home.

White makes spaces look bigger. While pure white radiates freshness and can feel cool, creamy tones will add warmth.

Blue conveys a sense of spaciousness. Bright shades are mood boosters, while darker hues are calming and create a feeling of security.

Grey, particularly if it is dark, makes the other colours in a room glow.

Shades of brown, especially terracotta and other earthy hues, add warmth to a space, while a pale, muted greyish-brown makes the interior timeless.

Nude, **blush** and similar **shades of pink** radiate friendly warmth. Their cooler hues make them modern and sophisticated rather than childish.

Red, the signal and alarm colour, makes clear statements, while shades mixed with grey or purple, such as mauve, are more muted and elegant.

Yellow conveys a happy vibe. When used in a deep, intense shade, it's best limited to a feature wall. A subtler shade, such as vanilla, brightens up dark corners.

Green brings nature inside. Calming shades like olive and sage generate a feeling of serenity, while bluer hues, such as mint green, brighten up spaces like children's rooms and corridors.

Left Will each room have its own colour concept or should similar tones be a common thread throughout your home? Why not create a moodboard for your entire living environment?
Below Colour fans show the most varied hues of a colour in a completely natural way, without being distorted by a computer screen.

THAT'S ME!

If you've seen the perfect teal in a magazine or feel that mustard yellow would be ideal on your wall, then get someone to mix your desired colour for you. Many DIY shops and specialised retailers offer this service, and can also answer all your questions about choosing colours.

HIT THE RIGHT *Note*

Natural hues, subtle powdery shades or perhaps different variations of green? These days, we're spoilt for choice. So how do you find the right colours?

There are plenty of ideas everywhere. You can flick through magazines and books or get inspiration online. Instagram and Pinterest, as well as lifestyle blogs and magazines, are packed full of suggestions.

With a moodboard, you can collect anything that catches your eye, such as impressive images, product photos, paint colours and wallpaper patterns. Whether digital or analogue, such a collage of ideas is a great way of creating and testing out mood effects. After all, it allows you to put together the most attractive combinations, but you can also discard them again in a jiffy. Be sure to also try out unusual or crazy combinations. The moodboard will reveal whether such surprising mixes will actually work or not. Test out and arrange things until you are totally satisfied with the overall look.

Colour fan decks are another practical tool, because they show the entire colour palette on narrow strips. Many paint manufacturers offer them for their product ranges, though Pantone and RAL colours are also available in charts.

If there are only a few colours on the shortlist, it is advisable to test them out in the room itself. Some manufacturers provide small sample tins, others offer sample cards. Testing the colours out on the wall itself will show how they change with the light. You will also be able to see whether the shades actually go with your furniture and floors. Everything looking perfect? Then get painting!

A colourful LIFE

Monja Weber
Kolorat

Monja Weber and Sebastian Alt founded their company Kolorat in 2015. Their mission is to offer high-quality paints for domestic use. They sell a wide range of beautiful, custom-mixed shades, and they also provide their customers with a host of tips and tricks. And if you're still unsure which shades best suit your home, you will find a great many tips and ideas as well as other services at their online colour consulting facility.

Left A smoky pastel blue with fine shades of grey has a fresh and stimulating effect without being overwhelming.

What is it that makes your paints so good? What's the secret formula?
Our entire range of paints offers high quality, excellent coverage and intense pigmentation. This ensures rich, vibrant products that don't need to be applied in umpteen coats. Not only is this practical, but it also saves time and money. Plus, our paints are eco-friendly. They are made locally, in Germany, and exclusively to order so there is no waste.

How many shades do you have in your catalogue? And which ones are trending right now?
The palette of paint colours at Kolorat encompasses more than 800 different colours. We can offer such a wide range because we have many different gradations of all the shades, ensuring that everyone is always able to find the exact hue they're looking for.

We're constantly monitoring what's trending in interiors, incorporating the relevant shades into our range and developing background colours that best complement the emerging interiors trends.
In addition to these trending colours, there are of course also the perennial favourites. These include, for example, grey and beige tones as well as white in all its gradations. Our customers currently have a particular penchant for all kinds of earth tones and darker blues, as well as blue or green hues which incorporate elements of grey. Warmer colours, such as salmon, apricot and our latest edition of terracotta, are also very popular at the moment.

My personal favourites right now include all shades of green, particularly the darker hues, and I'm equally fond of mud and sage. I also love cinnamon and coral. Depending on the space and its function, I like to contrast these with an intense blue. I enjoy combining different colours, because that's how a living space develops a great atmosphere.

you can also paint the ceiling. It won't actually close the room in, and will instead bring a sense of calm to the mix of tiles, bathroom furniture and ceramics. Good options here include dark green or even a soft grey-green, a subtle salmon or a warm beige.

The entry hall is a home's business card and is the first thing guests notice. You're not in this space for very long, however, so anything goes here – from bright and colourful to warm and cosy. If you've got kids or pets, you may want to choose a more robust kind of paint that easily withstands everyday wear and tear, such as dirty fingers or wet and muddy fur.

Why do you think that everyone's home should have colourful walls?

Feeling comfortable and at ease in your own home simply improves your quality of life, and colours play a major part in this. So many people just have plain white walls in their homes because they can't decide on a colour or keep putting off the idea of painting them.

It is, however, definitely worth just getting around to doing it – because nothing will change a space more quickly and more easily than a new wall colour, and it's also much cheaper to buy a bucket of paint than to invest in new furniture. If the finished look isn't ultimately what you were hoping for, you can simply repaint them. So it's definitely worth giving it a try.

Are there any colours that work best in a particular space?

As a general rule, colours reminiscent of nature have a relaxing effect and calm us down. Blue reminds us of the sky and sea, while green is good for the mind, and that's why a dark blue, a subtle greyish blue, a warm beige or a dark green are a good choice for our bedrooms –they are conducive to restful sleep. They also have a relaxing effect in busy family rooms. Bathrooms generally tend to be small spaces, which is why many people don't dare reach for any paintbrushes here. Yet, in addition to the walls,

What's important when it comes to choosing a colour?

You need to look closely. What colours are your existing furniture and fabrics, and what's the lighting like? I always advise customers to test their chosen colours beforehand using original colour sampler cards or a test coat.

What are the dos and don'ts when looking for colours and, ultimately, painting your home?

Follow your gut feelings and have the courage to use the colours you like. Just do it! And never stint on adhesive tape and covers – it will end up saving you a lot of work.

"

Everyone perceives colours differently.

Perc

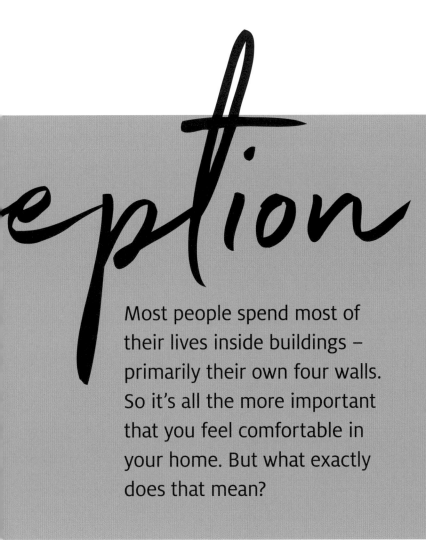

eption

Most people spend most of their lives inside buildings – primarily their own four walls. So it's all the more important that you feel comfortable in your home. But what exactly does that mean?

Whether you leave home early to head to your place of work or simply walk down the hallway to start your working day in your home office; whether you love being out and about exploring both your local surroundings as well as travelling further afield or prefer to spend time at home enjoying all your nice things – it's fair to say that we generally spend a lot of time within our own four walls.

And that's a good thing. After all, there's nowhere else in the world where you can feel quite as safe and secure, so completely accepted and relaxed, than at home, behind closed doors.

But what exactly is it that triggers these feelings of total comfort? And how do you make a home into the very best place in the world? These are two of many fascinating questions that are being examined by environmental psychology.

LIVING WITH ALL YOUR *Senses*

Feel-good living doesn't happen through the intellect. Rather, it is about the senses, perceptions and our living requirements, and this is why smell, touch and all the rest also need to come into play.

SMELL TEST!

A lovely fragrance is just as welcoming for residents and guests as a pretty bouquet of flowers. A mere subliminal tickling of the nose will more than suffice to trigger feelings of ease and comfort. After all, room fragrances stimulate the nerves, release hormones and influence perception. On thespruce.com you can find out how to make your own scents, whether little pouches or a spray.

With all my senses.

Right *There is no need for a candle or room spray – a simple eucalyptus branch fills the room with a fresh scent and looks pretty at the same time.*

Below *Just like pictures and knick-knacks, colourful home textiles can create a warm atmosphere, and pillows and blankets also appeal to the sense of touch.*

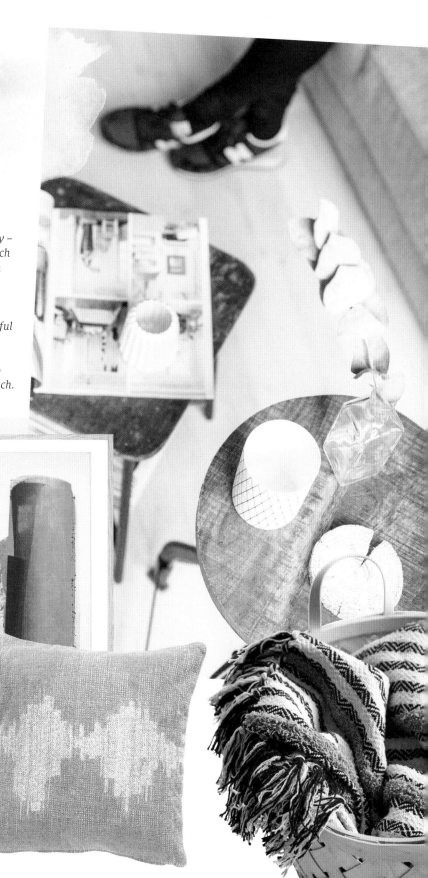

NOTHING BUT
Feelings

'I'm happy at home.' What does it take to be able to make this claim full of conviction? What is it that makes us feel wonderfully safe and relaxed, full of energy and contentment, in one particular environment and downright depressed in another? These perceptions are very specific to each individual. What makes one person happy can actually be off-putting to someone else. When it comes to finding out what your own feel-good home should look like, and how to create the happiest living environment for yourself, a little psychology won't go amiss.

Environmental psychology? Yes, this field of study does actually exist – and it provides fascinating, insightful information. Still a very new discipline, it focuses on human needs in relation to the living environment. Environmental psychology has nothing to do with feng shui, however. While both disciplines revolve around what makes people feel all-round comfortable in their immediate environment, feng shui is based on an Eastern philosophy. Its main mission is to make *chi*, or energy, flow freely through a building so that it can exercise a positive effect on the people who live in that place. Environmental psychology, on the other hand, is a Western discipline related to – and a subfield of – architectural psychology. The latter studies people within a structural context, and is therefore important for urban planning, whereas environmental psychology primarily deals with the home.

What criteria does a living space have to meet in order for humans to feel all-round comfortable within it? This is one of the key questions of environmental psychology, but the discipline also examines the interplay between humans and their living space. What difference does a living environment make, for example, when it comes to children's behaviour and development? What kind of environment do they – and adults – need in order to thrive and develop their full potential? After all, a home environment can be stimulating and inspiring, but it can also impede and even halt progress.

How does a home influence the way its inhabitants relate to one another? This is a question of interest not only to extended family groups,

Left Warm colours, a calm, friendly environment, natural materials – that's what relaxation looks like.

Left While some people listen and dance to their favourite music to unwind, others need a quiet retreat – and their knitting or crochet – to do so.
Below Bringing nature indoors is good for you – even if it's just a few pretty flowers. Here, simplicity and understatement add to the attraction.
Right If you enjoy creative pastimes, you should plan at least a small space for them.

but also to couples, flatmates and other people cohabiting. A space can trigger and intensify conflicts, but it can also ease and end them.

When it comes to interior design and furnishings, however, the focus is on a completely different aspect – living requirements. What do I want from my home? What am I looking for and what do I need there in order to function and be happy? These are questions of fundamental importance for improving quality of life, and they're equally essential for creating a feel-good home. Living requirements are closely linked with basic human needs. They don't have anything to do with design styles. If you know what you need for your home to make you happy, you can go with whatever style you prefer – be it rustic cottage and farmhouse, contemporary cool, minimalist, mid-century modern or Scandi chic.

Top of the list of such elementary desires for a home are the basic need for protection and a place of retreat, of light and warmth, the desire for a

place where you can be at peace and relaxed. These basics are the bare minimum for any home. It should be a safe haven that not only provides a roof over your head, but also protects you from the chaos and noise of the outside world.

The social component plays an important role too, however. After all, your own four walls need to be somewhere that meets your social living requirements. It's about being with others, about the desire for social contact, and for a space for your family and friends. Here, everything revolves around social interaction, communication and a feeling of belonging, yet the needs of the individual should naturally also be examined and addressed. The main focus here is on the requirement for personal development, recognition and a strong sense of self-worth. Last but not least, aesthetic preferences, such as a desire for order and structure, are another important factor to consider.

The exact way in which these needs manifest themselves obviously varies from one individual to another. Each person will have different priorities, and this is a factor that should not be neglected. While one person might love to withdraw from the outside world and switch off after a hectic day at work, another might need the lively family environment for stimulation and in order to recharge their batteries. One family member may like to listen to music, paint, read a book or pursue a craft in peace, and will therefore want a separate area to do this in. Another may prefer to spend their free time outside, and therefore will not need much space at home for their active hobbies. Some people like a bright, open and airy home, and as such prefer large, open spaces and views of the surrounding landscape. Others love being able to snuggle up and regard their home like a comforting embrace.

Top left Delightful fragrances
ensure that your sense of
smell will also perceive the
environment as pleasant.
Above A cosy snuggle corner is
a must for any feel-good home.
Far left A stool made of natural
fibres looks pretty and feels
pleasant to the touch.
Left It feels good to have lots
of beautiful things around
you at home.

WHAT DO
I want?

How am I supposed to know exactly what my needs are in terms of my living environment? This is a justified question, because most people barely give any thought to what they want from their home. Obviously, deciding whether to have a house with a garden or a flat with a balcony doesn't take long, and the number of rooms is a quick decision too – a master bedroom, a bedroom for each child and definitely a home office; a kitchen that opens out into the dining area and a living room that is spacious enough to fit the large modular sofa. But what else do you need?

One thing is for certain: working out your living requirements takes time. Listen carefully to your inner voice. What is truly important to you? Do you love life all around you or do you need precious moments of time alone? Do you prefer ample space for guests or rather for your hobbies? Would you opt for clear, orderly structures or a cosy, 'hygge' ambience? Thinking about all these aspects sometimes reveals some surprising answers.

It may be helpful to take a tour of your living space. Step into your house as if you were a guest. Examine everything closely. What triggers pleasant feelings, and which areas almost repel you?

Which colours or colour combinations appeal to your senses, and which do not? Fabrics, materials, furniture, but also room partitioning – look at it all consciously and take your time to note your thoughts. You're bound to come up with ideas for things you definitely want to change – whether it be moving an armchair or repartitioning spaces.

So you've created your very own perfect feel-good home? Excellent; but things can get difficult when two people move in together. It's not just a coming-together of two toasters, two sofas, two bathmats, all kinds of crockery and countless books. No, it might also be a clash of completely different living requirements and personal style preferences. So what happens now?

One potential compromise may be to set up a feel-good corner for each person, in line with their specific tastes. You'll get your cosy reading space with comfortable wing chair and floor-to-ceiling bookshelves, while your partner will have their super minimalist and hi-tech music area.

What's important is that each person gets what makes them happy and has their needs and desires met. If one partner suppresses their wishes and ideas to fit in with the other, there is likely to be conflict eventually – and it won't necessarily initially appear to have anything to do with the living environment.

Left Are you a bookworm? Then you probably won't feel happy without a lot of books and you should try to set aside space for a reading corner.
Below left If you're sharing your home with a pet, you should take their needs into account.
Below right And if you're working from home you should also try to make your home office as beautiful and relaxing as possible.

JUST LOOKING

The perfect worlds we see on Instagram and similar platforms may seem alluring, but if you try to copy other people's fancy homes, you can lose sight of your own needs. Social media is great for inspiration, but when it comes to your own home, what you want is all that counts.

Head
AND HEART

Stefan Suchanek
Neuro Aesthetics

Stefan runs a Munich-based agency specialising in neuroaesthetic communication strategies and awareness of form and effect. He advises clients on the layout of their office spaces, and also takes full charge of conceptualising and designing hotels and business premises – always from a psychological perspective. Stefan also shares his knowledge as a host, speaker and lecturer.

Stefan, you run an agency specialising in neuroaesthetic communications and awareness of form and effect. What do you offer your clients?
As an interior designer and business psychologist, I combine knowledge of both good design and behavioural economics. We're specialists in handling cases where space not only needs to be attractive and functional, but where the ambience and biopsychological response also play a key role for humans, clients, staff and the business as a whole.

A commercial space needs a certain allure and structure to maximise the chance of a potential client making positive purchase decisions while there; a restaurant needs an inviting atmosphere, coupled with warm hospitality and friendliness; a hotel needs to convey a sense of safety, security, appreciation and mental proximity; and a medical facility definitely mustn't trigger any sense of unease, stress or anxiety, but should instead have a protective, wellbeing aura for its patients. Ultimately, it's about a visual design that avoids any kind of stress and has a positive influence on our body and wellbeing.

What do you love most about your fascinating job?
I like making clients, students and anyone else who's interested aware of how our surroundings also influence our mind and soul. I can actually step inside the premises of a client needing help or guidance and immediately tell them where the deeper problem lies. I can also instantly feel whether a business will be successful or, sadly, not. No one wants to hear that, but that's what I'm there for. Then we make improvements and the clients, staff and success start coming. We need more beauty, charm and poetry; something that sparks joy, revives memories, creates appreciation and connection. Connection and happiness, in particular, are our future capital.

Left *Meaningful and sensual design can create trust, loyalty and bonding.*

Left *A feel-good home appeals to all the senses, including taste and smell.* **Right** *Familiar objects and rituals provide a feeling of security.*

into decisions by the latest social media trends or furniture catalogues.

How can we learn to heed our inner voice more when it comes to our personal living requirements?

We just need to be a bit more attentive, aware and humble when dealing with our surroundings, and leave our well-trodden comfort zone. Our brain needs little challenges without lapsing into stress – we've got enough of that already. We consume and copy far too much, yet create and act too little. If you've designed, built or renovated a piece of furniture yourself, putting in lots of love and effort, you're far less likely to be in a rush to throw it away. Because then we're being creators, not just consumers.

André Heller, whose sensuous works I really admire, made a lasting impression on me when he said the following words to me at an event. 'People can do a lot, people know a lot, but they have lost the ability to marvel.'

This has become my motto. Since then, I have been on a quest to find little or not-so-little moments or things that can amaze me. Suddenly, every day becomes exciting and satisfying.

What happens in our body when a space has an impact on us?

When it involves people, we talk of charisma; when it comes to rooms, we call it ambience. We can feel both, but they're both equally difficult to put into words. Our body releases hormones that influence our decisions. Adrenalin, for example, motivates us, while dopamine sparks joy and wonder. In a room, this hormone release can be triggered on a multi-sensory level, that is, through pleasant sounds or acoustics, through stimulating fragrances or ingenious shapes and proportions that encourage us to explore, through contrasts or the appealing use of colours, surfaces and textures – basically everything that makes up this magic or special ambience.

So what do we need in order to feel good at home?

Peace – with ourselves and peace with our third skin, which is our surroundings. This requires having spaces that make our lives easier and bring us lasting joy. Healthy colours, sustainable furniture, enough room for freedom and air, a few heirlooms as memories and, finally, even an expensive favourite piece that fills us with pride and makes our home our private palace, one we have created ourselves, without being pushed

The gut decision is based on love at first sight.

Order

No, it doesn't all have to be spick and span to the point of being clinical – but all of us need a sense of order if we want to feel at ease. So get ready to tidy up and enjoy a relaxed life.

Oops! Did someone just ring the doorbell? Quickly stack up all the magazines lying around, clear the hotchpotch of mail, shopping lists, keys and pens off the dining table and shove the basket of not-yet-folded laundry behind the sofa. After all, we get embarrassed when our guests are likely to see our mess – even though they themselves would probably barely notice it. There's a stack of papers on the desk, shoes, bags and jackets in the hallway, appliances, food and other random stuff on the work benches in the kitchen, and toy chaos in our kids' bedrooms – yes, every home has nooks and crannies in urgent need of tidying.

And it's worth making the effort to tidy up, because it's much easier for the mind and body to relax in a tidy home. If our surroundings exude a sense of calm, it will have an immediate effect on us.

Pretty little
HELPERS

The good thing about keeping things tidy is that the more stylish the storage devices, the more inspiring it is to put things back in their place. The range of boxes, baskets and suchlike on offer is huge.

INTO THE BOX

For a calm, uniform presentation on the shelf, the following rule applies: small items must not lie around loosely. Drawers, cupboard doors, boxes and magazine files are practical helpers. You can subdivide each area with partitions so that there is no chaos inside the drawers. That way, none of the smaller items get mixed up. Some things are best kept in labelled cans, jars or boxes.

Left The space under the beds is often wasted, but it can be put to good use with boxes. This bed box has been ingeniously filled with storage containers.
Top right A pretty wire basket is not only a useful storage utensil, but also a stylish accessory.
Far right A mix of open and closed shelving is ideal. This way, every item finds its own regular place and everything stays neat and tidy.

"
Stacks of
stuff – all
in good order.

Order makes Life
EASIER

In the morning rush of kids going to school and adults heading off to their place of work, something always gets left lying around – an unpacked textbook here, a half-empty coffee cup there and a solitary sock on the floor, having somehow lost its way. And in the evening? After a long day, it's often all the energy we can muster to clean the kitchen and gather up the dirty laundry before sinking into the settee, completely exhausted. There's no question that we often neglect a sense of order in our everyday life, pushing it down our list of priorities. It's totally normal and understandable. But it's also a shame; after all, having a tidy, orderly home is a much better way to live. External order translates into internal order. If our surroundings are clean and calm, we're more easily able to process our thoughts, our breathing gets slower and deeper, and we start to relax at last.

Disorder causes stress. Little piles of stuff here and there, and things flying around everywhere, stare us in the face like wagging fingers, constantly reminding us of what's still left to be done. This is true both for visible disorder and disorder that's hidden somewhere out of sight. While we may not constantly have to look at the chaotic mess of tools in the garage, the old clothes in the cellar or boxes overflowing with odds and ends in the attic, they do still haunt us in the back of our mind. Equally stressful are the rows with other family members because someone lost the torch, or left sports clothes scattered around all over the house, or didn't clean up their homework materials. The time needed to look for things that are lost or mislaid is equally irritating – and too precious to be frittered away. Not to mention all the money that is wasted on buying duplicates or groceries that end up well forgotten and well past their expiry date somewhere in the far recesses of the kitchen cupboard.

Order relaxes us. When there's nothing that disrupts our view, when there's no chaos that makes us feel uncomfortable, when everything is in its assigned place, then there's no stress. Any anxieties that we may bring home with us dissipate much faster in surroundings that are calm, peaceful and tidy, and all the household tasks also become easier when everything is readily to hand. In short, order makes us happy.

Left Floor-to-ceiling built-in cupboards make optimal use of the available space and are visually unobtrusive.

For a home to be orderly, everything needs to have its very own permanent spot – whether it be toys, clothing, kitchen appliances, party decorations or any of the numerous other things needed in a household, from pens to spare toothpaste. It is also important, of course, to put things back in their place immediately once used.

So a tidy home needs enough storage space to ensure all possessions can be stowed away. It's a good idea here to turn even unused nooks and crannies into storage space. You'll be amazed at the options you'll find under stairs, under sloping ceilings and in little alcoves. Sometimes you'll discover furniture items that were just made for that particular spot, and other times it's worth having shelves and cupboards custom-made for this purpose so that these spaces can be utilised efficiently but also in a visually attractive manner. These two aspects – using the available space efficiently and ensuring the storage

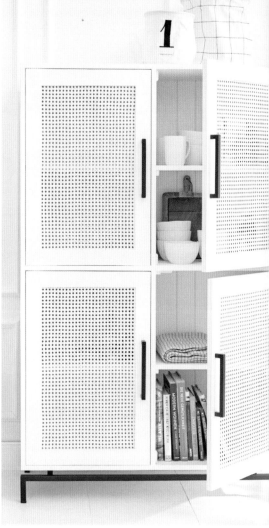

Left Soft storage baskets, pretty mugs or shapely jars are wonderful containers for pens. *Above* Woven panels make cupboard doors look airier and lighter, yet they still hide everything from prying eyes. *Right* If you want more serenity on your bookshelf, just sort the books by cover colour. To go one step further, turn the books around so it's not the backs but the white pages that show.

Far left *A closed shoe rack puts an end to chaotic trainer storage, and perhaps there's even enough room for gloves, scarves and hats.*
Left *You can display some of your favourite things on long, wide shelves.*
Below *In this prime example of a perfectly employed utility room, the space under the work surface is used for laundry baskets, and the space above for detergents and cleaning agents.*

space blends in harmoniously with the rest of the decor – are particularly important, because if cupboards, shelves, baskets and boxes are stylish, tidying up and keeping things in order become much less of a chore and much more fun even at a visual level.

Open or closed? This is one of the fundamental questions when it comes to storage space. Closed doors are a great way to keep less attractive stuff stowed away and out of sight. A floor-to-ceiling cupboard extending from one corner of the room to another and painted the same colour as the wall will be unobtrusive while still providing lots of space. Of course, things should be kept tidy even behind the closed cupboard doors! Open shelves, on the other hand, create an airy, filigree look, but this aesthetic only works if the individual compartments are not overflowing with stuff, and are instead kept tidy as well as neatly sorted. Attractive baskets and boxes can store additional odds and ends and anything else you don't want to be seen.

AT THE
Home Office

Once the chaotic mess of pieces of paper strewn across your desk starts hampering your work, you know it's time to tidy up. The advantage of having an orderly workspace is that it allows all your thoughts to flow freely and unimpeded. Nothing is getting in your way – both literally and figuratively. There are no bits of paper, Post-it® Notes, pens or wires cluttering up your desk – nor are there any distractions blocking your creative flow.

An orderly home office is not just designed to help you work, of course. It's especially important to keep this space tidy if it's sited in a living room or bedroom. It looks better, and you'll feel more relaxed when you knock off for the day if you don't have to-do lists and stacks of work staring you in the face.

If you want to keep your workspace permanently tidy, the best way to start is by having a clean-out. Go through all the papers, leaf through old folders, binders and magazine holders, rummage through all the boxes and crates. Be thorough and only keep what's truly important. While you may be able to put old documents in the rubbish bin, this is not the case for official certificates, tax documentation and suchlike. At the same time, put your filing system to the test. Does it work well for you or would a different system be better? Old magazines, invitations and so on can similarly head to the wastepaper basket. Open box files are good storage options for magazines which you want to keep for a little while longer. You're only interested in fruit tart recipes? Then make a baking folder and stick them in there. The rest of the magazine can be recycled. Try to be as rigorous as possible, and make sure everything you're keeping is being filed away sensibly. Not only will this free up space in cupboards and shelves, but you'll also make it easier for yourself to instantly filter out all future documentation.

Since we rarely have time to go through invoices and other important missives on the spot, it's helpful to have a folder or filing tray to put the mail in initially. Once you've completed the task, the document will continue its journey – either to the wastepaper basket or a designated folder. Odds and ends like hole punches, pens, file fasteners and printer paper are best stored out of sight in drawers or closed boxes. The writing utensils you're currently using can be kept in an organiser on your desk.

A good, tranquil feel in your study requires calming aesthetics. Invest in folders, magazine holders, boxes, box files and crates that have a uniform appearance. Not only will this make your shelves look tidy, it will also make them look more attractive.

Left If your work corner is open to the living room, you should pay extra attention to keeping it in good order.
Below left Why not make the wall above the desk look pretty? After all, it's what you'll be looking at every day.
Below right Some shelving systems allow you to assemble the individual elements to taste.

ON CLOUD 9

If you want to do without paper, you can digitise all your important documents and save them on a hard drive. A practical alternative is the Cloud, which you can access from anywhere and which automatically synchronises the data – it's also a good idea for storing your photos.

Less
IS MORE

Lilly Koslowsky
stilles bunt

Can colourful ever be calm? With Lilly, it can – because her life is hectic and, you guessed it, colourful, but her home provides the necessary serenity to balance things out, with clean lines and lots of light. It works because Lilly has a passion for interior design – and is a master of orderliness. She also draws on this talent to help others tame their chaos and create a stress-free family life.

Left Everything that is visible on the shelf should be arranged in a tidy and orderly fashion.

Your home is designed in Scandi style. What do you love about this particular interior design?
I love Nordic cleanness and the space this style liberates. For me, many aspects of Nordic interior design provide the perfect, low-key basis for my personal understanding of leading a life of practical and embodied minimalism.

What exactly is embodied minimalism? Could you please explain it to us?
Minimalism is often associated with bare walls and empty spaces, but that's definitely not my personal idea of it. I have translated the general principles of minimalism for our everyday life and our lifestyle, and it's primarily about conscious decision-making and mindfulness. Basically, less stuff means more time! If you've got less stuff to clean up, maintain and care for, you simply have more time for other things. Like life. Children. Your relationship. Less physical stuff means less stuff in your head too – which is incredibly liberating. Less stuff also means fewer things you have to clean – less laundry to be washed, dried and folded, and fewer knick-knacks to dust.

What does order mean for you?
For me, order starts in the head. A lot of it is about working on mindset. My order structures, rituals and routines provide me with a sense of security and ensure clarity both internally and externally. To a certain extent, I've definitely always been someone who loves orderliness, but that doesn't mean it's automatically easy to maintain. Fortunately, however, we can learn how to do that. My most important guiding principle that I also share with my mentoring clients is: perfection is overrated! What's important is establishing methods and systems that fit with your own everyday life and that are also sustainable over

Left *A shelf on wheels can be taken to wherever it is needed and put out of sight when it's not in use.*
Right *The same applies to the wardrobe – sort and throw out regularly to keep things tidy.*

liberating. Afterwards, it's time to take stock and work out the requirements for each individual space. Many furniture items should ideally be able to store things and it's perfectly fine for them to serve multiple purposes, particularly in smaller living spaces. If we have a certain basic order, a system that we can rely on, it's easier for us to maintain order on a daily basis and make our home a feel-good space. The groundwork here definitely starts in the head, however. Then, keeping things orderly externally ceases to be quite so difficult.

What are your top 5 tips for creating and maintaining order?
1. Step one is always to declutter.
2. Anything left after that needs to be given a permanent home.
3. Once you've established a certain basic order and systems, you'll have laid the foundations for long-term order.
4. Habits and routines help you consistently maintain good order.
5. The two-minute rule: if it takes less than two minutes, do it straight away!

the long term. In our family, I am definitely the order freak. My eldest daughter has inherited a bit of that obsessive tidiness from me. We have established systems in our everyday lives that make it easier for us to maintain order as a family, and that takes a huge amount of stress out of our everyday family life.

Do you have any special tips for minimalist living Lilly-style?
A good mix of cleanness, cosiness and ample air to breathe – for me, that's what makes a space a feel-good place. My top tip: remember that not every empty space needs to be filled, nor should you pack a room with pieces of furniture and decorative objects without being clear about how you want to use this particular room in your everyday family life.

And how do we achieve the order we need for enjoying a relaxed life, either alone or when sharing our home with others?
I firmly believe most people simply have too much stuff. I certainly don't mean to be judgmental here; all I'm saying is that chaos and disorder are often also a result of excess and overabundance. It's really helpful to do a thorough and truly genuine decluttering, because it's incredibly

"

Order conveys tranquility – inside and out.

Sense

# of Touch

Hands off? No way! Touching is in. Whether rough or soft, cool or warm, fluffy or silky – surfaces stimulate the sensors in our fingertips, creating moments of intense comfort and pleasure.

The sense of touch is something we engage in actively while exploring our surroundings with our fingertips. Countless receptors feel a surface and register its temperature, texture and solidity. Does it feel cold, smooth and moist? Then it could be the wet tiles in a shower. Does it feel warm, soft and supple? Then it's perhaps some yeast dough on its way to the oven. Sometimes the fingertips even discover a little more than the eyes. In the case of a child's feverish forehead, for example, they cannot be beaten.

The fingertips are organs of touch, but it's actually the entire skin surface that feels and senses things. A soft sweatshirt or a warm woolly jumper? The skin on our neck and arms will recognise it instantly. So if you want to satisfy all your senses at home, you also need to be mindful of your sense of touch.

FOREVER *Feeling*

Sometimes an object's surface is so alluring, we just have to run our hand over it, again and again. This is precisely the appeal that every home needs in order to ensure our sense of touch is satisfied too.

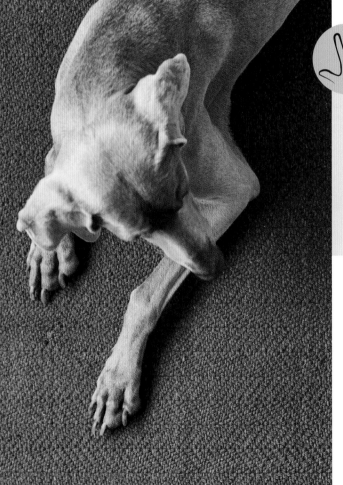

PET YOUR PET

Living with pets is great for many reasons. One of them is the fact that cuddling your dog or cat, your rabbit or even your guinea pig reduces your stress. If you lovingly stroke a pet's soft fur for a while, this will lower your level of the stress hormone cortisol, allow your heart to beat more slowly and thus lower your blood pressure. An all-round healthy experience!

Left *Even a furry roommate loves a nice and cosy home.*
Top right *You can probably never have enough blankets. Fine virgin wool can be a little scratchy for sensitive people; alpaca and cashmere are much softer.*
Right *Almost as exciting as the combination of colours is the mixture of materials that is used in furniture, surfaces and home accessories.*

"
It's about pleasing the hands and the eyes.

That feels so LOVELY

Our fingertips are constantly in use, and register their surroundings with a similar degree of attention to our eyes. When we're typing on our keyboards in the home office, when we're peeling and chopping vegetables for lunch, when we're tickling the cat on the sofa or when we're hanging our freshly washed laundry out to dry, our fingertips are constantly touching different surfaces and textures. Sometimes these are nice and smooth, other times they have interesting textures, for example there may be fine grooves or rough graining, a continuous pattern or random dips and bumps. Surfaces can be hard, soft, supple, crumbly or fibrous. Just like the eyes, our sense of touch also loves different textures and fascinating contrasts, and it, too, likes to be challenged. So a feel-good home doesn't just offer a variety of materials and textures to please the eyes, but also constantly provides exciting experiences and familiar sensations for the fingertips and the skin in general.

Left *Velvet is a fantastic material for cushion covers, and linen makes for an exciting contrast.*

Surfaces like those found on cupboards, work areas or even walls and floors are an enthralling arena for our sense of touch to play in. They are explored with our fingertips, but also with the soles of our bare feet. Walking around on a fluffy carpet early in the morning eases you into the day, while stepping onto bathroom tiles will wake you up more abruptly. When you walk barefoot on stone, concrete or floating-screed floors, they feel similar to how they look – cool and hard – which, in summer, is very pleasantly refreshing. They give a space a modern look and can even have a slightly worn finish in loft homes. A small rug in front of the sofa or under the dining table, or a long runner in the hallway or entrance area, give these floors a warmer all-over feel – and also change things up a bit for the soles of our (bare) feet. Timber floors, whether using wide wooden boards or parquet style, not only look warmer and softer, but they feel it too. Pale wood always works in any space, whereas dark floors are more classic and elegant.

Walls play somewhat less of a role when it comes to our sense of touch, but they can still be designed to provide some variety. Granite in the bathroom, a coloured glass panel as a stove splashback, and exposed brick around the chimney, for example, feel

Far left *Go barefoot more often. This is not only good for the sensory system of the feet, but also for your sense of touch.*
Left *Upholstery covers should always be easy to care for.*
Below left *Solid wool and wood are a great partnership.*

good and add character to a space. Fabrics are also important teammates. They are as pleasing on the skin as they are to the eye, bringing comfortable warmth and cosiness into the home. Carpets and rugs lay the foundations for this. Those made from natural fibres don't just feel good; they also provide a pleasant sense of homeliness. They are an interesting contrast to hard floors and, on timber floors, further emphasise the comfortable, homely ambience. In larger spaces, they can define specific areas. For example, a large Persian rug under the dining table separates this area from the lounge area. Woollen rugs are not only warming, but they are also easy-care, because the wool's natural greases make them relatively non-sensitive. Whether these are woven or shag pile, patterned or single-coloured, is purely a matter of taste. Cotton rugs, especially colourful rag rugs, are particularly well suited to children's bedrooms, kitchens, hallways and bathrooms, because they are easy to wash if they get dirty.

Fabrics of the vertical dimension also play an important role as drapes and blinds. Heavy curtains convey a sense of security and serenity, while light, flimsy ones billow and dance in the wind, creating a fun, carefree ambience in the room.

Cushions, pillows, blankets and throws are the main fabrics we're in constant contact with. The fluffier they are, the more tempting it is to run our hands over their soft surface.

Cool, casually creased linen is particularly pleasant on the skin in summer, simultaneously conveying a sense of ease. Velvet, meanwhile, looks sumptuous, while felt is more rustic. Wool and corduroy captivate with both their cosiness and their texture. If the yarn is particularly thick and the stitching particularly large, they attract curious fingertips as if by magic – and the eyes will naturally also enjoy beholding such gorgeous crafted pieces.

Home accessories with hard, smooth or even rough surfaces, on the other hand, make for interesting contrasts against all the soft fabrics. A metal lampshade, for instance, or an earthenware jug, a terrazzo pot or a vase made from Murano glass will not only look exceptionally decorative in your home, they also add attractive highlights to the space. And, much like worry stones, they entice us to keep touching their pleasant surfaces.

Left Smooth ceramic and textured upholstery are here united by the colour scheme.
Above The sense of touch also plays a role in crockery. Do you prefer smooth and shiny or matt surfaces? A combination of both is also exciting.
Right Pillows and blankets with a raised pattern tempt you to explore them with your fingertips.

FURNISHING
Material

The main players in the space, however, are not walls, floors, fabrics or accessories, but rather the furniture itself, and because we're in constant contact with it, for example when we sit down to eat, work and clean up, it also needs to feel good. Chairs, sofas, cupboards and tables also have something to offer the receptors in our skin. Of course, they not only need to feel good to the touch; they have to be functional and tailored to the needs and wishes of the resident or residents too; not to mention the fact that they need to be attractive to look at and to genuinely enhance the home.

Many natural materials feel good overall. The different types of timber, for instance, don't just have fascinating graining; they're also gloriously smooth when you run your hand over them, and even more so if the piece of furniture has been soap-treated, waxed or oiled, and this particular feel isn't hidden under a thick coat of varnish. An oil, soap or wax finish doesn't just feel velvety smooth; it also allows the wood to breathe, creating a pleasant indoor climate.

Whether it be maple or oak, pine or walnut, wood is almost always the material of choice when it comes to building furniture. It is stable, durable and easy-care, adding wonderful warmth to the interior design and blending in pretty much everywhere. Importantly for any creative DIY fans out there is also the fact that second-hand wooden furniture offers endless possibilities for (re)design projects.

Natural fibres, like rattan and reed, not only feel good, but also convey a certain sense of ease – be it in the form of a cane sofa or cupboards made from Viennese mesh. Wool, on the other hand, makes everything soft and cosy – and not just visually. Virgin wool is an extremely robust, non-sensitive material for upholstered furniture, whereas linen is an airy, lightweight fabric for summer chair covers, and leather is the classic option for armchairs and sofas. It feels pleasant and ages beautifully with dignity and a patina.

Metal and glass offer very different feels to these soft natural materials. The coolness, hardness and smoothness of brass, stainless steel and iron can accentuate a space with rustic or sophisticated accents, fitting just as easily into an industrial style as they do a modern, minimalist look. We particularly see metal in tables and shelves, often in combination with glass. On its own, it is often used as a robust frame for seats, tables and shelves. In kitchens, professional chefs appreciate the hard-wearing nature of stainless-steel workspaces, and if it looks too cold, timber makes a good partner.

Left The metal lamp, the leather armchair, the wool-covered sofa and a cosy fur make for a tactile feast!

Below left Of course, a piece of furniture should not only feel good, it should also look good.

Below right Wood and metal in straight, angular shapes ensure a clean, clear look.

CERTIFIED OK

Sustainably produced furniture is made from renewable raw materials, under fair conditions and without long transport routes. They are non-toxic and ideally recyclable. When buying furniture, go for FSC certification. Choose FSC 100% over FSC Mix where possible.

***Right** Good design also pays attention to the subtleties, such as the leather holders here for the cushion.*
***Below left** Gentle curves and a filigree frame – does a chair need any more to be simply stunning?*
***Below right** Clear lines and a simple design – furniture with a timeless look will accompany its owner for a lifetime.*

OLD STUFF

Some classic designs are still produced today, others are now only available second-hand. The best starting points for finding such a piece are the classified ads, flea markets, auction houses and estate liquidations, as well as junk and antique dealers.

FURNITURE
Design

Furniture needs to be eye-catching, while also blending seamlessly and harmoniously into the home. Timelessly attractive yet somehow also in vogue – and of course it needs to perform its function perfectly, while being long-lasting, robust, flexible, sustainable and eco-friendly. There's no question designers face a long list of requirements when creating new furniture pieces.

Yet purchasers have a similarly long list of criteria to think about when deciding on a new bed or new shelving unit. Function is naturally of fundamental importance. Is the table long enough for the big gatherings of family and friends? Will the cupboard fit all the clothing or might a chest of drawers have to help out? Are the shelf's compartments big enough for records and large coffee-table books? Will the children's bed be able to handle the odd bout of bouncing and romping around? Materials are another important aspect – because they play a major role not only in the visual side of things, but also in terms of durability and robustness. What's the point of having the most solidly made armchair if it just doesn't look right?

Design is a similarly important selection criterion. Much like in architecture, new styles have constantly been developed over decades and centuries. The twentieth century was especially formative for modern-day furniture design –n materials such as glass, metal and MDF came into the equation, chairs began to 'float' and industrial design became acceptable in living rooms. The Bauhaus movement reduced furniture to its basic concept, while the 1960s and 70s produced completely new forms. While some ideas vanished back into oblivion, others remain permanent and expected fixtures in international furniture design to this day.

So what about today's furniture fashions? In many areas, including lifestyle, there's a 'back to basics' movement happening. Think plain, simple and functional, yet featuring very harmonious shapes and natural, easy-care materials. We expect modern furniture to be produced sustainably wherever possible, with a view to being environmentally friendly and also being long-lasting. As such, it perfectly complements the design classics that are still commonly found in many homes.

So many of the concepts conceived by the great designers of the twentieth century have aged wonderfully and, thanks to their timelessness, look just as modern and contemporary as they did when they were first produced. A feel-good home can easily be a fusion of these and the latest brands – and it is indeed this mix that makes for well-rounded and interesting interior design.

MADE FROM *Good Wood*

Lasse Lund Lauridsen
Form & Refine

The three founders of this Danish label are passionate about Nordic design in its simplest form. Not only is the design of the furniture, accessories and fabrics clean and timeless – it's sustainable too. Lasse, who's responsible for the commercial side of the business, is particularly fond of wood, and likes his oak furniture oiled or soap-treated. For information on this label, visit formandrefine.com.

What do you love about your job – and about furniture?
I love creating a well-designed piece that appeals to customers, offers top quality and is in keeping with the times. I particularly like wooden furniture. The warm aesthetics and sense of touch are just wonderful. Making a piece of furniture is a lot of fun. Jonas Herman Pedersen is the designer in our trio, but we're all involved in the process and make joint decisions about the direction we want to take. Of course we love the pieces we've designed ourselves, but I also like many of the classics, such as Kaare Klint's Safari Chair, with its lovely use of wood and leather or canvas.

You guys place great emphasis on sustainability. Tell us a bit about that.
Yes, that's important to us on many levels. With the wood, for example, we work a lot with oak. An oak tree stores a lot of CO_2 in its lifetime, only releasing it when its wood is burned or rots. So when we work with its timber, it still continues to bind the carbon dioxide. And we're of course constantly planting new trees too. Oak is also a sustainable material, because the wood is so timeless and long-lasting. The furniture pieces are made for eternity. We're mindful of sustainability with other materials as well. Cork, for example, constantly regrows, and our canvas is made from recycled materials. We don't want to work with plastic, because it's just not that easy to reuse. Alpacas produce wool for their entire life, and there is no harm done to the animal when it is sheared. Alpaca wool is excellent quality, very robust, easy-care and long-lasting. We work with a co-operative of 30 alpaca farmers in Bolivia. And we don't just buy our wool from them, we also make sure it's actually produced by them.

Left Cuddly and soft on the skin, and wonderfully relaxing on the eyes.

a long time. The quality has to be right, and the furniture must be durable and long-lasting. And if its design is timeless, the piece can be used and loved for many years. It is also nice when a piece of furniture can fulfil different functions in a variety of locations. A wooden bench, for example, can stand at the foot of your bed to accommodate your clothes at night or under a window as a raised stand for your pot plants. People tend to move house more frequently these days, and any piece of furniture should therefore be flexible enough to find its place and function in the new home.

What is your tip for the care and maintenance of a piece of wooden furniture?
That will, of course, depend entirely on the desired surface treatment. If the piece is oiled, its care is easy and straightforward. All you need is soap, sandpaper and oil. The soap ensures that the surface becomes clean. If you find any fine scratches or small stains, you can gently remove these with fine sandpaper. Then you oil the surface. You can apply two or three coats of oil until the wood is fully saturated. After this treatment, your piece will look as good as new.

What do you find fascinating about Scandinavian design?
It is minimalist, has a certain clarity and coolness, but thanks to the use of natural materials it is not cold or uncomfortable. Many people who visit us always say that everything looks so tidy, but in fact that's just the style – less is more. Plus everything is beautiful, but also has a purpose. This external calm is transferred to people and calms the soul. The use of natural colours also contributes to this relaxed atmosphere. No flashy colours, only hues that come directly from nature, such as terracotta, undyed cowhide, linen or natural wood, possibly with white pigmentation. All these materials not only look good, they also feel good and are very tactile. There is also the typically Danish way of having not just one, but many lamps in every room. I really appreciate that. We have many different light sources in each room – table lamps, floor lamps and wall lamps. With two lamps you feel comfortable, and four lamps light up the table while you eat. Candles also provide this typical cosiness.

What makes a good piece of furniture?
A good piece of furniture must be good at fulfilling its purpose. For example, you have to be able to sit well on a chair, sometimes even for

High-quality furniture appeals to all five senses.

Performing a live concert at Madison Square Garden!

The boys
are back
in the Big Apple!

THE STROKES

ONE NIGHT ONLY | APRIL 4, 2011

JULIAN CASABLANCAS The SINGER ALBERT HAMMOND JR. The GUITARIST NICK VALENSI The OTHER GUITARIST
NIKOLAI FRAITURE The BASSIST FABRIZIO MORETTI The DRUMMER ELVIS COSTELLO The OPENING ACT

Listen up! If you want to feel all-round good in your home, you need to optimise your soundscape. It means blocking out external noises and filling your space with sounds that are beneficial for your soul.

Acoustics is the study of sounds. How are they created? How do they spread around a space and move from source to receiver? These and other similar questions are what acoustics specialists seek to explore. This field of research is centred on noise pollution and how to avoid it, which is why acoustics also play an important role in designing our living spaces. After all, we need to do all we can to reduce any disruptive background noise and to optimise sound. Noise stresses the body and should be minimised where possible in a feel-good home.

So how do you go about blocking out external chaos, bustle and noise or at least reduce acoustic stress? And how do you ensure that the sounds you really do want to hear – from deep andmeaningful conversations with loved ones to feel-good music – sound particularly good in your house?

THE BEST *Sound*

Acoustic background music from morning to evening or a very personal selection of music for special hours? Listening habits differ, but everyone should enjoy the best sound possible.

SPOTIFY LIST

Life at home is just so much better when you can also enjoy the perfect soundtrack. That's why Marion Hellweg has put together the perfect feel-good playlist especially for this book. You can download it directly via this QR code . . . Listen and enjoy!

SINATRA *The Hits*

Left, above and right *It doesn't always have to be the biggest speakers. You can now find elegant little boxes that transmit big sounds, and if you prefer not to disturb anyone around you, you can simply put on a headset. Noise-cancelling headphones are ideal for deep relaxation.*

To live without my music would be impossible to do.

Great Sounds
NOT NOISE

Sound moves through a space in waves. It causes the air molecules to vibrate, changing the air pressure – and our sense of hearing can perceive this. The modified air pressure is also known as sound pressure, and it determines volume – the greater the sound pressure or pressure fluctuations, the louder we perceive the sound to be. Pitch, on the other hand, depends on the frequency of the pressure fluctuations. The higher the frequency, the higher the tone sounds. Pitch is recorded in hertz (Hz) and volume in decibels (dB). A feel-good home is of course also all about minimising any extraneous noises that may disrupt the sense of relaxed harmony in a house.

It is important for a home to have good acoustics for the wellbeing and health of all the people living there, because noise isn't harmful only when it's loud. Quieter noises that persist for long periods of time can also feel irritating, and even harmful. For the body, any noise equals stress. So it's all the more important to ensure it is not exposed to elevated levels when in its own four walls.

Trams juddering past, lorries screeching to a halt, motorbikes roaring past and drivers honking their horns – all to the sound of humming engines, the occasional ringing of bicycle bells and children laughing or shouting on their way to school. If you live in a city, you're right amongst all the hustle and bustle, and you are lucky to have cinemas, restaurants and bars within easy reach. The flipside, however, is having to deal with negative aspects like traffic noise.

Conversely, only those who live far out in the countryside are able to enjoy the rustling of the trees, the twittering of the birds and a great sense of tranquillity. This peace and quiet is the perfect soundscape for relaxed living, where you hear only noises you're making yourself. There is plenty of beauty in your life. But even in tranquil surroundings, noise can still disrupt the serenity. From a dripping tap, to a neighbour hammering or sawing, a cock crowing his heart out or a heated discussion in the next room – there's always some rumpus going on somewhere. Yet everyone perceives things differently. What one person finds annoying may barely cause someone else to flinch. So people's sensitivities

Left Large windows, in combination with stone floors and walls, can worsen acoustics in a room. Carpets will help.

vary. Nevertheless, we should strive to achieve a calm home with good acoustics. So how can we reduce noise levels and block out any unwanted sounds? Having a calm, quiet atmosphere is restorative and not only good but essential for concentration – particularly in the bedroom, as well as the home office and living room. Before you resort to any major structural work, however, it's worth trying out a few simple solutions. Windows can be a weak area when it comes to noise. Soundproofing through double-glazing will block out much noise, but is not easy to install – especially if you are a tenant rather than the owner. New window seals, however, as well as insulation for blinds are easy to fit. Soundproof curtains also help create more peace and quiet in the bedroom. Not only do they block out noise, but they also absorb the sounds generated inside the room, making for good acoustics. The same approach used for the windows can be applied to the door; new seals are incredibly effective at muting noise, and draft excluders can cover the sound and cold air gap under the door.

Of course it's not just about blocking out unwanted external noise. There are also a few things you can do within your own four walls to improve tone, because good room acoustics are essential in any feel-good home. Poor acoustics mean noises – whether caused by humans or machines – reverberate around the room for longer. There's basically an annoying echo. Noise levels particularly tend to get unpleasantly high when several people are talking or noises come from different corners of a room. Modern structural designs can favour such a long-lasting echoing sound. Large, open rooms with high ceilings and building materials such as concrete, ceramic tiles, metal and glass all ensure that such an echoing effect may be created.

Above An acoustic panel on the wall not only helps to improve the sound, it also spices up the look of the room. The upholstered furniture and the carpet will also help.

Far left Smooth wood panelling on ceiling, walls and floor is attractive and makes for a good ambience, but it needs silencers.

Left Carpets not only keep your feet warm, they also reduce the noise level.

Left Bare walls and a smooth screed floor, metal furniture and no curtains make for an acoustic nightmare. Chair cushions and a carpet are first steps towards a better indoor climate. Wall panels also go very well with this style.
Below Fabric lampshades are a good idea for the acoustics in stairwells.

GOOD NIGHT!

Your home's ceiling and floor are concrete, and the walls have minimalist built-in cupboards? That's the perfect place for noise to go berserk. To nevertheless ensure your relaxed sleep, you could replace the headboard with large fabric-covered panels to reduce noise levels.

MUFFLING
the Noise

Hard materials cause sound to ricochet and fly back and forth through the room like an echo, with no buffer, and naturally this is bad for good acoustics in your home for these can only exist when the noise is deadened. That's why it's a good idea to opt for soft materials with porous surfaces.

Don't worry – you don't have to undertake any major renovation that involves changing the look and feel of your home. Even small changes to the interior design can make a major difference. In general, the more spartan a room is, the more problematic acoustics can be.

Fabrics are a quick hack for achieving good acoustics. Curtains on floor-to-ceiling windows deaden noise even when they're not drawn. And on the floor, carpet can make a huge difference, reducing not only reverberation time, but also footstep noise. The thicker it is, the more it absorbs noise. Thickly upholstered furniture isn't just extra comfortable; it's also a good sound-absorber. If you're a big fan of leather sofas and wooden or steel furniture, it's worth your while to add a few cushions, blankets and and throws. In addition to the extra level of cosiness they provide, these accessories will also help mute any background noise. Similarly, fabric lampshades will bring a much better result for your acoustics than their glass or metal counterparts.

Large, bare walls fling any noise back and forth between them, while properly filled bookshelves make for perfect sound-absorbers. Wall tapestries will also deaden noise. Posters behind glass panes, meanwhile, will reflect sound much more intensely than pictures painted onto canvas.

If you want to be on the safe side, you could opt for so-called 'acoustic pictures' that have been specially produced to absorb sound. Whether printed with a motif or as colourful elements in varying shapes and colours, there's a wide range of solutions available. Taking things one step further, you can try affixing acoustic art panels to your walls and ceilings; they are best custom-made for your space. Arranging narrow slats, generally made from MDF, on these surfaces fractures the sound and reduces noise levels.

Listen
TO ME

Marion Hellweg
Interior Designer

Not only does this journalist, author and interior designer live in a cool renovated flat in a historic old building, but she's made a career out of it too. As editor-in-chief of Living & More *magazine, she offers her readers the best home ideas and tips, and she's also packed her know-how into countless books. If you're struggling to find the right style for your home, you'll find her advice online or follow her on Instagram* @marionhellweg

Left Vinyl discs decelerate your life and your musical perception. Listen to them to celebrate special moments.

Why would the author do an interview in her own book? Because it's a topic she's passionate about – she can't live without music.

Marion, are you one of those people who have music going in the background from morning till night or do you regularly need times of quiet?
I actually almost always listen to music that fits my mood or what's going on that day. Songs with the right beat and lyrics, but I wouldn't call it background music, because melodies significantly influence my mood and emotions. There's a tune for every minute of my life – it's very, very rare for me not to have music playing. I never listen to the radio; I don't like listening absent-mindedly to stuff controlled by others.

What sort of music do you like?
My taste ranges from jazz to heavy metal, but my absolute favourite genres are punk, hardcore, metal and alternative. 'My music' is music that's honest and authentic. Music that conveys the artist's feelings and message, and touches me in some way. This could be sad and melancholic songs or happy and cheerful ones. For me, it's all about the overall package of lyrics plus sound. If I can feel it deep within me, then it's good. That's when it touches my soul.

Your podcast BÆM is also about music – but that's not all you're talking about, is it?
My podcast is a passionate project of the heart. I sit at my kitchen table and talk to people I find interesting – people I really like and who have something to tell us. Of course we talk about music, but we also talk about other things – about art, love, our mindset and the highs and lows of life, and as we do so we don't beat about the bush, we're frank and BÆM always gets straight to the point.

Left Marion only uses her headphones to listen to music when she wishes to shut out the world and switch off.
Right Pretty cool, these modern devices. They beautifully blend in anywhere.

cassette collection, which I listen to occasionally. But that's more of a nostalgia thing. Plus there's something very appealing and atmospheric about putting a record on. Time somehow seems to slow right down when you drop that needle, sit back in your leather armchair and make a conscious decision to listen to a record.

What would you say is the best way to listen to music? What are your tips for an optimum listening experience?
At home, it's best to listen wirelessly, so you can easily control the music via voice command or on your smartphone or tablet. I'm not a fan of headphones in everyday life, because they cut you off too much from the outside world. So the absolute must here is to splash out and buy the best speakers. If you do want to retreat a bit, however, and there are other people around you, headphones are a great option.

You can put speakers in every room, wherever you want. They're often small and portable, so you can position them exactly where you need them most – and because they're so stylish, they won't detract from the interior design either.

What does music do to people? Why is it good for us to listen to music?
Music moves us. It touches us. It gets us dancing and makes us cry. For me, music is my best friend. It's someone who always listens to me, understands me, comforts me and motivates me – no matter what I'm going through in life. In short: music is my home. And I want to share this feeling, which is why I used to compile mixtapes for people I care about. Even today, I send my friends songs or make playlists for them to show them I'm thinking of them and to hopefully brighten their day.

Hence the Spotify playlist?
That's right. My 'Feel Good' list contains a great selection of fantastic songs that are good for the soul. After all, a feel-good home isn't just about aesthetics – it's also about the music that provides the perfect backing for it all.

Now, the podcast is digital ear candy, but how else do you listen to music?
I stream it. I consume music the same way everyone else does. I'd say I discover 20 new artists and three times as many new songs every week. Of course I still have my old record and

Spotify Code for the 'Feel Good' playlist

Where words fail – music speaks.

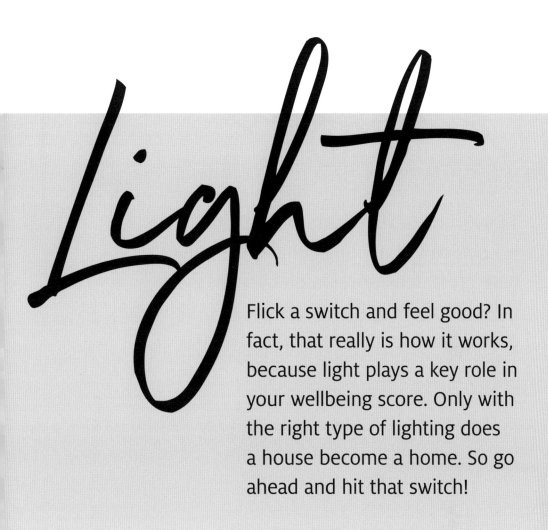

Light

Flick a switch and feel good? In fact, that really is how it works, because light plays a key role in your wellbeing score. Only with the right type of lighting does a house become a home. So go ahead and hit that switch!

Daylight has a fundamental impact on all of us, on our general wellbeing as well as our efficiency and vivacity in everyday life. After all, we're much more energised after jumping out of bed when the first rays of sunshine are already filtering in than when we have to crawl out of the covers before dawn. Our mood also improves when we're surrounded by more light – not only outside, but also indoors. A home that gets lots of natural light through large windows therefore scores high on the feel-good scale.

Light works not only during the day but also even when it's pitch dark outside. While strategically placed artificial light sources cannot replicate the positive effect of natural daylight, they can create a cosy, cheerful or intimate atmosphere that improves the mood. So the choice of lighting, and its positioning, is hugely important in any feel-good home.

Beautiful
LAMPS

There's no question lamps are practical, but in addition to their functional value, they also have great decorative potential. A glass or metal pendant light? A shade made from wood or perhaps paper? There are many options.

Anyone
who does not
believe in
miracles
is not a realist.

Audrey Hepburn

ON THE MOVE

A stylish little lamp for reading while snuggled up on the sofa, or on the patio table while you are barbecuing, or as a decorative piece on the sideboard? Without inconvenient cables, flexibility is no problem. Portable battery lights go wherever you need their beautiful glow. In addition, many lamps can also be dimmed so you can always ensure the best atmosphere.

Left *Concrete base, metal insert, glass cylinder – modern lights bring diverse materials together.*
Top *The light source does not always have to be hidden under the shade. Fancy lightbulbs with ingeniously twisted filaments are eye-catching.*
Right *Pendant lights hung in small groups above the dining table provide good light – and put themselves in the spotlight.*

"

More than just a useful appliance.

Nice and
BRIGHT HERE

Light moves in electromagnetic waves. The range between ultraviolet rays and infrared rays is particularly important for us, because it's actually visible to the human eye. The unit of illuminance, or 'luminous flux' per unit area, is measured in lux, which is based on the Latin word for light. No creature on earth can survive without light – after all, it's an elementary part of photosynthesis, which is how plants produce oxygen.

Light has a tremendous impact on our body and mind. It ensures we're alert and feel active when we wake up in the morning, ready to start our day, and tired as we sink into bed at night when the daylight slowly fades. While our internal body clocks tick differently from one person to the next, they are certainly influenced by light. Dull days and darkness can make us feel down, even slightly depressed, the so-called 'winter blues'. Some people even suffer from SAD – seasonally affective disorder.

Sunshine, meanwhile, boosts our mood. It's no coincidence that many people are active and full of beans in summer, but quickly lose motivation when the days draw in for winter. And is it any wonder – after all, during the shorter winter days, our body only receives a fraction of the light it is exposed to on sunny summer days. While a sunny day can have a lux reading as high as 10,000, this will only amount to a mere 3,500 lux on cloudy days. So, whenever possible, it's important to make the most of the sparse daylight to go for a walk even in winter – not only to enjoy some fresh air, but also to ensure you're getting enough light because sunlight improves our mood and physical activity, as well as making sure the body produces important vitamin D.

Yet not all light is the same. There are significant differences between natural and artificial light. Both the spectrum and the intensity of daylight are greater than those of artificial light, and the latter also lacks natural dynamics. Put simply, colours can be perceived in greater detail in daylight. Reading in natural light is also more pleasant, because we are able to make out the text more easily, thus not straining the eyes. Nor do our bodies produce sufficient vitamin D for bone strength in artificial light.

It is possible, however, to use a well-thought-out lighting scheme to control the atmosphere in your

Left With large windows and partition walls made of glass, nothing stands in the way of the incoming daylight.

home and create all kinds of different ambiences at the flick of a switch. There are just a few things you need to bear in mind.

Pleasant, easy-to-live-with lighting requires functional lighting on the one hand and and mood lighting on the other. After all, you want your work spaces to be well lit, without making them look cold and uncomfortable. To strike the best balance between these two different aspects, use a mix of different light sources. Make sure there is ambient lighting and functional task or work lighting, then add the odd extra lamp for stylish and characterful accents.

Ambient lighting will illuminate the whole space unobtrusively. It's essentially the foundation for turning dark into light. This can be achieved by a ceiling light or even a wall light. Indirect light, such as from an uplight, is nice and soft, low-contrast and non-glaring. But it's not suitable for reading or working, because it strains the eyes.

Left A good reading lamp makes it much easier to peruse a book. If the light comes in at an angle from above, the pages won't cast any shadows over the book.

Above Bedside lamps don't always have to stand on the bedside table. If there is a lack of sockets or simply not enough space, you can let them dangle from the ceiling instead.

Right Pretty lights in simple sockets are optically so backgrounded that you can easily fix a few more of them above the table.

Far left When the sun shines, they look quite inconspicuous, but as soon as the twilight sets in, candles come into their own. They will conjure up a wonderful atmosphere.

Left As a rule, pendant lights should always hang high enough above the tabletop for you to easily see each other while you are seated.

Below Why not let a lamp take the stage for once? This one is bound to steal the show.

This is where functional work lighting comes in. A reading lamp provides good light for burying yourself in a book, while two pendant lights above a kitchen workspace help you see what you're doing when you're chopping vegetables, and a desk lamp provides light when working from home. These practical aids illuminate specific areas to help us with our tasks.

Additional accent light sources are the ones that create a distinct feel-good atmosphere – a standard lamp in the corner, for example, or a table lamp on the sideboard or shelf, or a pendant light hanging low over the side table. Much like candles, they create little islands of light and cosiness – albeit with a different kind of brightness. This mood lighting is of course not a must-have, but you'll see that it makes a world of difference. Quite apart from their natural talent in creating atmospheric brightness, these lights seem to physically move pictures on the wall, furniture, decorative objects or simply themselves into the right light.

Right A mirror above the sink is extremely useful, and if you position it well, it'll also reflect the daylight.
Below left If you place your desk at right angles to the window, you'll get natural light from the side – perfect for screen work.
Below right Floor-to-ceiling curtains will also put smaller windows in the limelight.

CURTAINS UP

Here's a little curtain primer. Net curtains and voiles are airy and allow light into the room, while protecting privacy. Heavier, often lined curtains are chosen as drapes or over-curtains that block out the light and keep the heat in the room. Then of course you may prefer blinds . . .

PLEASE
Come in

Daylight is the most pleasant and most natural form of lighting, which is why you should let as much of it as possible into your home. Large windows or perhaps even a floor-to-ceiling glass façade and glass terrace doors as well as front doors with glass inserts are all ways of allowing a lot of natural light into spaces, while at the same time providing a good view of life outside your own four walls without being obtrusive.

If a room has only a small window, or indeed no window at all, it doesn't mean you can't have any natural light. A skylight above the room door or even a glass insert in the door will bring in light from the room next to it. A window strip – that is, glass inserts in the wall shared with the adjoining room – is another way of transforming the trapped darkness into a much brighter space, with the added bonus of making the room look bigger too. These sorts of internal windows could sit in a horizontal strip directly under the ceiling or be installed as a narrow, vertical wall element, for example right next to the door. Or how about another idea: why don't you replace a whole solid wall with a metal or timber-framed glass wall?

Glass bricks were long frowned upon as dated, but today they are back in fashion. These bricks have the advantage of letting daylight in, yet still blocking

out the curious glances of others and therefore preserving your privacy. The roof can also be opened up – windows in slanted roofs let in ample light and a glass roof ridge with transparent sides will allow a lot more sun into the upper level of a house.

Giving the staircase an open design will see more light filter into the different levels, and this works particularly well when there are skylights in the ceiling above the stairs or the banisters are filigree or even transparent.

Using mirrors is another useful trick for brightening up small or dark spaces. These essential living accessories are especially helpful in long corridors, bathrooms and even bedrooms. If you hang them opposite a window or glass door, they will reflect the incoming light, immediately making the room look much larger and brighter.

But what if you want to actually block out sun and daylight? Curtains are the easiest way of darkening windows. Not only are they practical, they also act as decorative elements that are easy to replace when you want to give your home an entirely new look. Roller blinds and pleated shades are similarly flexible, and can be used if there's no space for panels of curtain material either side of the window. Venetian blinds have adjustable slats to regulate the amount of light coming in, and the same goes for internal window shutters.

LIGHTBULB
Moment

Daylight is wonderful, but sometimes the light coming through the window simply isn't enough. By the time night falls, we're switching on our artificial lights, and an additional light on the desk or in front of the bathroom mirror can also be very helpful during the day if the weather is cloudy.

In the past, all you had to do was put a new lightbulb into the socket, but traditional lightbulbs were largely taken off the market in recent years because they use too much energy. Fluorescent tubes and energy-saving lamps with electronic ballasts are also now being phased out. In these more energy-conscious days, if you want to buy lightbulbs, you'll most likely be choosing between halogen, LED and energy-saving lights without electronic ballasts.

One important selection criterion here is luminosity. While this was formerly stated in watts for filament lightbulbs, the unit in use today is the lumen. Watts denote energy usage, whereas lumens describe luminosity, that is, brightness. So the higher the lumens, the greater the light intensity.

Conventional lights generally differ in terms of brightness – but they also differ in light colour and energy-efficiency

category. The warmth of a light – that is, the colour temperature – is stated in kelvins. The higher the number, the whiter and colder the light. Halogen lights tend to be a cold white, which works very well in workspaces and anywhere that needs to be well lit. In living rooms and bedrooms, however, they usually create a cold, rather sterile, uncomfortable ambience, not to mention the fact that they don't last anywhere near as long as their LED counterparts.

LEDs are today often the light of choice, being very energy-efficient, extremely long-lasting and also dimmable. They do not generate heat either. LEDs come in all shapes, sizes and colours. They can radiate holograms or be used in fairy lights indoors or outdoors. When in the form of metre-long strips, they can enhance furniture, walls, ceilings and floors, changing colour whenever you wish. They can also serve as candle substitutes, flickering in paper bags and other highly flammable decorative elements. And of course they can also light up rooms in the form of a lightbulb – in any conceivable shape or colour temperature.

As the name suggests, energy-saving lights are generally more economical. They do, however, need a few seconds before they reach their actual maximum degree of brightness. Plus, after their use, you will need to dispose of them in hazardous waste facilities because of their mercury content.

Left The light should be a little brighter above the kitchen worktop. Here four lamps are in use.
Below left Placed in a niche, this light creates a cosy ambience by the bed and doesn't blind you when you're reading.
Below right If a lamp stands in the limelight, it can be a little more extravagant.

NICE 'N' SMART

Wandering from lightswitch to lightswitch is so yesterday. Today you can control your lighting by radio or voice command. This works with individual Wifi-enabled lamp devices, but also with entire lighting systems that are connected to an intelligent control centre.

LORD OF THE *Lights*

Steffen Salinger
Artemide

In 1960, Ernesto Gismondi and Sergio Mazza founded their lamp manufacturing company Artemide. Just seven years later, they received an award for their Eclisse table lamp. Over the decades, this now globally active company has produced countless design icons, though Managing Director Steffen Salinger has retained a particular fondness for the Tizio desk lamp since his student days. artemide.com

We cannot live without light. But what exactly accounts for the special fascination with lighting in our own homes?

In view of the fact that nearly 80 per cent of all sensory perception is visual, light is the element that has the greatest impact on our perception. Light enables us to actually experience qualities such as size, shape, texture or colour in the first place. In addition, light has a major impact on how we feel – I find that rather fascinating. The right choice of lighting and light sources contributes significantly to our wellbeing and health. The right lighting improves our concentration, our overall relaxation and the quality of our sleep. This is also where the Artemide 'The Human Light' philosophy comes in. Lighting from Artemide always follows the requirements of the room and the needs and activities of the people within it.

What, then, makes for good lighting and what should we pay special attention to?

Good lighting always adapts to the spatial conditions as well as the individual requirements and activities of the user and should therefore be flexible and interactive. In order to best meet all the different needs, dimmable lights with different light colours are necessary. Most of the Artemide bestsellers and innovations, for example, can be controlled and configured intuitively with the Artemide app. The intensity and colour temperature of the light can be changed quickly and preset light scenarios can be called up. When building a house or renovating an apartment, special care should be taken to plan the lighting in good time. If you know early on which light you want to use where and for what purpose, you can take the position of cables, switches, dimmers and sockets into account when carrying out the electrical work and save yourself costly conversion work later on.

__Left__ Design object or work utensil – in the best scenario, a lamp can be both.

as atmospheric lighting for comfortable hours around the dining table. You absolutely need a lamp on the desk in your study or workspace which imitates daylight with its cool light and keeps you awake and alert. The light from the computer screen alone is not sufficient. The bedside lamp in the bedroom, meanwhile, with its warm, white light, should promote the production of melatonin and thus prepare you for the sleep phase.

Lamp manufacturers now rely almost exclusively on LEDs. What are the advantages of these light bulbs?

Thanks to dynamic, smart LED systems that can easily be controlled via an app, you can significantly reduce your energy consumption. The lighting can also be precisely adapted to your particular needs as a user. With LED lighting, the changing daylight can be accurately simulated, which has a positive effect on our wellbeing. In addition, the small size of the LEDs opens up completely new design possibilities. Design, light quality and energy efficiency go hand in hand with LED lighting.

Is there a minimum number of light sources that a room needs?

As a rule of thumb for illuminance, which is measured in lux, around 100 lux is required for the living room and hallway, and 300 lux for the kitchen and bathroom. Illuminance is not the only criterion, however; the light colour, the quality of the colour reproduction and avoiding glare are just as important.

An ideally composed lighting scheme takes into account different room zones and illuminates individual areas differently. Pendant lights, ceiling lights and wall lights with indirect lighting are generally well suited for lighting the living room, but are rarely sufficient on their own. When reading or watching television in the evening, it quickly becomes clear that other light sources are needed. Table and floor lamps are particularly suitable as supplements here. Several small light sources that are not too bright can create a pleasantly relaxing ambience.

A good example of a room which needs more than just general lighting is the kitchen. Here you will be cooking, eating and spending a relaxing time with family and friends. Therefore, in addition to the basic lighting, a brightly lit work surface is required for cooking as well

Light plays an enormous role in a room's spatial effect.

A touch of green makes life much more enjoyable. It's healthier, cosier and more relaxed. Housemates of the plant variety aren't just stylish accessories – they offer all kinds of other benefits too.

Nature is good for the soul. It's no surprise that forest bathing has become a worldwide trend. The sound of rustling treetops, the thick canopy of leaves swaying protectively overhead, feeling the soft soil underfoot and inhaling the fresh, woody air – with every step, every glance and every breath, stress simply fades away and new energy flows through your body. And both the eyes and mind have a chance to rest.

Obviously, not everyone enjoys the luxury of owning a lush jungle in their own home. Yet it's true: those who surround themselves with houseplants end up living a better life. You don't need to create a primeval forest, not even a wildflower meadow. A simple fern sitting on the windowsill or an umbrella plant on top of the chest of drawers, culinary herbs in the kitchen or a bird-of-paradise in the sunny corner by the sofa will suffice – and they look great too.

Urban
JUNGLE

Whether you display miniature trees or hanging plants, cacti or sculptural showpieces – houseplants are attractive and will enhance any room, especially when they're presented in stylish planters and baskets.

EYE-CATCHERS

The same rule that applies to other decorative items in the home also holds true for plants: small specimens look much better if they're not stranded alone but arranged in a group of at least two. If you have sufficient space, you could even create a little indoor garden, perhaps with a plant or two suspended from the ceiling. Large plants, however, can handle the limelight on their own.

"
You'll soon get the hang of it!

Left Plant boxes don't just look nice on a balcony. The long-legged versions can also be positioned anywhere in the house.
Above Sturdy clay pots and baskets create a natural country cottage ambience.
Right Succulents are extremely easy to care for and generally quite robust, plus they make for extravagant eye-catchers.

LIVING
a Green Life

Not everyone is lucky enough to be able to unwind from everyday stresses in their own back garden, on a generously sized balcony or terrace, or in a vegetable plot, to be close to nature, rummage around in the soil and – most importantly – sit back and watch the green shoots grow. Yet gardening isn't just an outdoor thing; you can also do it inside your home. After all, nature thrives just as well on a window ledge, on a shelf or in the corner of a room.

A mini indoor oasis adds charm – and also improves the climate in your home, because every single plant is a remarkable little air purifier. And this is how it works: a plant uses the green chlorophyll in its leaves and the available sunlight to convert carbon dioxide into precious oxygen, releasing it into its surroundings. In addition to this injection of fresh air, every plant also increases air humidity because most of the water it is given is filtered and released back into the ambient air. This makes plants perfect for creating a pleasant

indoor climate, especially in the winter months when the air is dry from heating and irritates the mucous membranes in your nose. As a general rule, the more biomass there is, the better the atmosphere in a room. So for extra-good air, choose plants with the largest possible leaves. These include the trendy-once-again Swiss cheese plants, soft green African hemp, philodendrons and flamboyant giant taro or upright elephant ears.

In a bedroom, some of these verdant air purifiers even improve our sleep. While many plants temporarily stop working in the dark, mother-in-law's tongue, aloe vera and orchids remain active even at night.

Some indoor plants also take on a job as cleaners and filter toxins from the ambient air. Such toxins do exist – they are generally found because construction materials, furniture, carpets, dyes, cleaning agents and suchlike all release formaldehyde, benzol and other unhealthy substances into the air without us even realising. In bedrooms, living rooms, studies and children's rooms, your very own urban jungle is able to absorb these evaporated toxins and purify the air. The mother-in-law's tongue and weeping fig are prime examples of plants that are particularly good at filtering chemicals from the

Left *Today it's here, tomorrow there – a tea-trolley mini garden can be moved to wherever you like in the room.*

Far left In this bedroom, a fiddle-leaf fig creates a pleasant ambience and a calm background.
Left This lovingly assembled green still life imbues an unused corner of the room with life and charm.
Below An extravagant Swiss cheese plant, with all the makings of a superstar.

environment, although ivy, peace lilies, dracaenas and dieffenbachia will also do a good job and create a healthy indoor climate.

It's not just the air in your rooms, however, that benefits from your very own botanical garden. The greenery also helps us relax – on every level. Taking care of things is a basic human instinct. There is something almost meditative and incredibly fulfilling about plucking off a withered leaf here, adding a bit of fertiliser there, and giving the larger leaves a dusting. For a brief moment, office strife and children's tantrums are tuned out, and you're just happy to sit back and watch your little green charges grow and thrive.

In addition to a sense of happiness, plants also help you relax because of their sound-proofing abilities. Just as thick hedges can reduce street noise in the garden, large, thick leaves can also muffle indoor noise. Rubber plants and Swiss cheese plants are particularly good at this.

And it won't just be your ears that will thank you; you'll also be making things easier on your eyes if you live the green life. Smartphones, tablets, computers and TVs – we're constantly staring at screens. The blue light puts a strain on the eyes and the brain, while social media algorithms fray our nerves. Regular breaks are a must. Instead of being glued to your screen, why not admire the sight of your little green friends – it's good for your eyesight and will clear your head.

Left Small green cactuses instantly get more attention if they are planted in multiples.
Below Plants are particularly charming when the room's dominant accent colour – here a powder pink – is mirrored in the flower pot.
Right The hanging shelf and a chest of drawers become ad hoc exhibition spaces for this collection of a wide variety of cacti and other succulents.

So what's it going to be – small and delicate or large and striking? Sun from morning to night or a shady, north-facing spot? There are green-living options for everyone and every situation. If you've got green fingers and love plants, you'll take good care of your floral housemates and can confidently surround yourself with high-maintenance exotic and sensitive plants. Yet there are also suitable low-maintenance plants for those who have neither the time nor the inclination to dedicate themselves to indoor gardening activities, and who just want to pick up a watering can every so often and be done with it. Mother-in-law's tongue, for example, is a succulent and only needs a bit of water every few weeks. It's a similar story for elephant's foot, also known as ponytail palm, which doesn't look much like either an elephant or a hairdo but quite resembles a palm tree. Devil's ivy lavishly trails its way down to the floor in a shady corner, and aspidistra doesn't need much light or water to thrive either.

Left *Tone on tone – flowerpots don't have to be identical to look good in a group, but similar colours and materials help to visually unite a diverse plant family.* **Below** *Don't forget, it's important to repot figs and other greenery in larger containers every few years to ensure that your plants will grow and thrive.*

NURSERY

You'd love to have more than one specimen of a particular green beauty? No problem. Many plants are easy to propagate from cuttings while others, such as spider plants, produce their own offspring. You can find tips for propagation and care at www.homesandgardens.com

CARING FOR
Plants

Most plants don't demand much attention in order to thrive – light, water and fertiliser will generally result in lush growth. There are a few things, though, that you need to remember.

Not every houseplant loves sunlight. Some prefer semi-shade or feel most at home in a dark corner. And, similarly, they have preferences when it comes to watering. While some plants get really thirsty and like to be drenched several times a week, others need only a small drink of water every now and then. A lushly flowering plant will demand regular fertilising, while cacti don't need added nutrients anywhere near as often. When buying plants, make sure to take note of their needs and preferences and choose the right one for yourself and your location – it will make them so much easier to look after. You'll enjoy sharing your home with lush green friends who visibly feel right at home.

TIME OUT

Can you feel it? Anyone tending to plants automatically unwinds. Whether you're getting your hands dirty repotting a plant or carefully plucking off withered blooms – when your attention is focused on your floral housemates, the constant stream of everyday fears and worries stops and your mind clears. Our tip: indulge in a meditative break.

Any living plant that's flourishing and thriving will eventually need more space, which is why you need to repot your houseplants into larger containers once every few years. Not only does this give their roots sufficient room to spread, it also provides them with fresh compost and nutrients. Ideally you should go for peat-free compost to protect the wetland ecology. Self-watering pots are a practical idea – they help ensure that your plants will be watered regularly, while saving you one or two rounds with the watering can yourself.

Many plants are dormant in winter. They take a break, needing less or no fertiliser, and generally also less light and water. If you are mindful of each plant's individual needs, they will start into spring with renewed fervour after their period of hibernation.

KING OF THE

Jungle

Igor Josifovic-Kemper
Happy Interior Blog

Happy living. It's only fitting that someone who's passionate about this topic should call their digital home the Happy Interior Blog. Igor has been writing about beautiful homes, travel, good food and plants – the very essence of a happy life – since 2011. He shares his love of houseplants in this and two other books, and as the Urban Jungle Blogger. To find out more, visit happyinteriorblog.com and urbanjunglebloggers.com or find him on Instagram @igorjosif.

Left *Spotted or striped leaves, jagged edges or smooth ovals – houseplants come in all shapes, sizes and colours.*

What exactly is it that you find so fascinating about plants?
Plants bring life into your home, because they're a part of nature that we can let thrive within our own four walls. I find most spaces without plants empty and devoid of life. Yet just one single plant can change this impression. The colour green, which we encounter in nature, always triggers a feeling of tranquillity and security within human beings. Aside from this general sense of wellbeing, plants also improve air humidity and purify the air within our homes.

When did you first fall in love with plants? Or have you always had green fingers?
I think my love of plants goes right back to my earliest childhood. I vividly remember that we always had plants in our home, and some of them were very large indoor plants indeed. I didn't see them as decorative items, but rather just as natural components of our living space. Even when I was a university student, I always owned at least one plant that moved with me from one student flat to the next.

And what does your home look like these days? Are you a plant collector?
Well, there are plants in every room of my house. I have accumulated a wide range of different species – from the classic Swiss cheese plant to rare specimens such as *Philodendron billietiae*. My largest plant is a *Philodendron selloum*, which is a good two metres high and has giant leaves. It really is a jungle plant! In fact, you could probably call me something of a plant collector, but I try not to go overboard with my passion. I travel a lot, and my lush housemates need to be able to survive without my close attention. That's why I try to keep the number of my green companions down to a manageable amount.

Left With its triangular leaves and extravagant colour, false shamrock adds a touch of the unexpected. *Right* Green goes anywhere – on the windowsill, suspended from the ceiling or surrounded by piles of books next to the settee.

For example, a minimalist home becomes way cosier with a single statement plant, while a boho-chic interior lends itself to a mini jungle of a variety of different plants.

What are your best plantcare tips?

The most useful tip is to get plenty of information about each plant! You should always find out all you can about your green companions – that way, you'll know exactly what they do and don't like. Do they want to be watered frequently or not so often? Do they prefer lots of light or a bit more shade? Do they need high air humidity or are they more partial to dry surroundings? Once you're aware of all their likes and dislikes, you can avoid any major mishaps.

Which plants would you recommend to a beginner? What are some of the robust all-rounders that thrive anywhere?

Many different plants are low in maintenance and robust, including traditional favourites such as Swiss cheese plants, mother-in-law's tongue, devil's ivy and spider plant. Corn plant and peace lily are also very undemanding indoor favourites.

So what do you do with your houseplants when you're away on longer trips?

If I'm away for longer periods of time, I get a good friend to stand in as my plantsitter. She'll even send me the odd photo or video while I'm on holiday, so as to keep me updated on my plants. If I'm going on a shorter trip, the plants can easily get by on their own. The day before I leave, I just make sure I inspect them all well and give them sufficient water.

How does one get started with plants? What are the main dos and don'ts?

There are no real rules. If there's something you like, then it's good for you. The most important thing to bear in mind is the needs of each plant when it comes to location, light, moisture and temperature. Once you're clear about their preferences, you can go completely mad. You can, of course, follow the conventions of interior design and play around with height, size, leaf pattern and colour. That's how you create attractive, well co-ordinated plant arrangements.

Is there an interior style that works best for plants?

I think plants fit any style and any home. It's more the number of plants that makes the difference.

"

My favourites are plants with extra-large leaves.

Special

Spaces

'I'll stay here forever.'
There are places that are just
too beautiful ever to leave.
Nowhere else is quite this good.
So it's all the more important
to create such special spaces
in your own home.

Sunlight streaming through a leafy canopy overhead, soft moss underfoot, woody aromas tantalising the nostrils and rustling sounds in the undergrowth – for some people, secluded forest clearings are their favourite places. Others, meanwhile, prefer jetties that extend out to sea, where they can squint into the sun reflecting off the water and listen to the waves lapping against the pillars. Personal special spaces can, however, also take the form of a seat by the window in a small café, a chair in front of your favourite painting in a museum, a bale of hay in a field or a bench on top of a hill that overlooks an entire valley.

Special spaces are a source of both energy and relaxation. They're the spots where we can recharge our batteries and process our thoughts for a while – which is why everyone needs at least one such private haven, and that includes inside your home.

Comfort
WRIT LARGE

Special spaces can span multiple areas or consist of just a single seat. No matter how many people are sitting here, the furniture needs to be comfortable enough so that no one ever wants to get up again.

GOT IT COVERED

Living your life surrounded by natural materials is simply better for you and, of course, this also applies to your upholstered furniture. Covering fabrics such as wool, linen and cotton are not only sustainable, they are also hard-wearing, easy-care and pleasant on the skin. A leather sofa can also quickly become a favourite place – and over the years it will acquire more character.

" No wish to get up again — ever!

Far left A comfortable sofa is not complete without blankets and cushions.
Left A good armchair envelops you like a warm hug.
Above The bed can be a special space too, made snuggly with a bedspread during the day.
Right No sofa should ever be without a coffee table. After all, where else would you place candles, coffee and your book?

IT'S WHERE
I like it best

A home is obviously designed to be the place where you unwind and breathe a sigh of contentment as soon as you step through the door. It's of course also where you recharge and come up with creative ideas and where your mind and body can let go and relax. That's the whole point of a feel-good home, isn't it? Yet it's also where everyday life dances its daily tango. Stress and arguments, a chaos of toys, dirty laundry, non-stop appointments and housework are all part of normal life, and while they naturally all need to be dealt with, they often don't make us feel happy. Quite the contrary – everyday challenges often drain us and cause anxiety, and sometimes we simply don't want to focus only on the more trying things and tasks; we also want to intersperse duty with some fun and mood-boosting, or just retreat and take a breather – basically we all just enjoy some time out.

This is exactly why everyone needs their very own special space in their home; a place where they can unwind and recharge; a small corner where everything is harmonious and they're surrounded by nice things and their favourite memories. What happens in this particular space is entirely up to each individual.

Your special space could be your yoga mat that sits waiting in the cupboard for you to roll it out once a day in front of the large bedroom window that overlooks a lush park. Your special space could also be the bathtub where you can enjoy some time out, surrounded by candles and buried under mountains of fragrant froth; where you experience a sense of relaxation on several levels with the help of scented bath oils. Even the old armchair heirloom in the corner of the living room could be your special space, not only because it's perfect for reading and listening to music, but also because you can simply let your eyes wander and take in what is going on around you. The kitchen may also be your special space – at least if you are able to switch off as you chop, stir, season and taste. The same is true about a little desk in a hallway niche, because it gets the creative juices flowing as you look out at the sky. Some people like using their special space to pursue their favourite hobby – as a place where they can knit, read, paint, cook, meditate, write poetry, listen to music or start the day with a sun salutation undisturbed.

Left The details make all the difference. Plants, candles, cushions – make sure your special place is nicely fitted out.

Other people, meanwhile, just enjoy
looking out of the window or around
their home. They take in the colours
and materials surrounding them, the
feeling of warmth and security in a
particular armchair in a particular
place, the way the daylight filters
through the window, or the furry feel
of their cat, who likes to curl up on
their lap in this snug little spot.

Special spaces are also places of
power. They can provide you with new
energy and relieve you of everyday
stress and worry. They're a haven of
tranquillity amidst the business of
day-to-day living – the refuelling stop
for relaxation and a good mood. It's
this place of power that you can return
to at the end of a hectic day to shake
off all your pressures and to recharge
your batteries. Alternatively, it may be
the place where you start your day and
from where you set off fully charged to
face the world and its trials.

In short, a special space is just that –
it is yours and no one else's; it provides
you with exactly what you need; and
it's up to you to make it special.

Right Relaxation and pleasure go hand in hand, so drinks and snacks are must-have accessories for special spaces.
Below left Often, it is quieter in the bedroom than in the living area. So how about a little 'me time' corner there?
Below right Once everyone has gone out, it's even lovely and quiet at your favourite dining table.

SUBTLE SCENTS

The nose also plays a role, and not only for those whose special spaces are centred around the stove. Scented candles, aromatherapy oils, fragrant flowers or even fresh coffee all help you to relax and get in a good mood, a signal that this is the ideal spot for you to take a little break.

JUST *Me*

A refuge, a place to recharge, a haven of tranquillity, a source of inspiration, a corner to unwind – quite simply, a special space is something different for everyone. You may already know exactly which nook is your absolutely favourite place in your home. That's perfect. If you generally like your home, however, but don't really have much of an idea which area is your special space, get up now and go to look for it.

Walk through your home, listen carefully to all your senses and seek out any potential special spaces. Is there a room where you feel particularly comfortable and safe? Where for no obvious reason your mood improves and your stress hormones drop? Then go and examine it a little more closely. Where do you feel particularly at ease? It might be an armchair or sofa, the window seat at the dining table or the wide windowsill, the bathtub or the unused nook in the dining room that would be perfect to become your own exclusive creative corner. What is important, however, is that this space is located where your gaze cannot wander over the yet-to-be-sorted laundry or the stack of paperwork.

Your home may not be particularly big and may not have any nooks or areas to retreat to, but that's not a good reason not to devise a special space. Instead of a physical boundary, you could make a time limit. Explain to your family that the reading chair is your domain in the evenings; or that you don't want to be disturbed when you roll out your yoga mat by the balcony door early in the morning. Headphones are a clever way of blocking out the world and being present just with yourself.

What's important to you? What do you like? What gets you excited? Collect ideas and inspiration to design your special space exactly as you want it to be. A moodboard can help here. Whether in digital form or as a real-life pinboard, a moodboard can bring all these ideas and inspirations together into a unified whole. You can include fabric and colour samples and pictures of furniture, carpets and lamps that you have found, as well as photos of beautifully designed places to recharge. If it feeds your soul, it belongs here. Once you have enough material, simply filter out anything that doesn't quite fit. Take as long as you need to move things around and rearrange them until you're really happy with the end result. Then it's time to make it all happen in your home.

Turning a special space into a perfect place of recharge means filling it with positive energy. You can do this by surrounding yourself with some of your favourite things and letting go of all negativity. Establish pleasing rituals and soon you will find that a sense of relaxation sets in even when you just think about your special space.

ALL
Together

One person goes to piano lessons, the other to volleyball training. The third one heads to the office and the fourth to see her girlfriends. In a family, everyone does their own thing, and their activities can often be quite different and lead them in very different, even opposite, directions. So it's all the more important that all the generations regularly come together at home to chat, eat and play. After all, it's about encouraging cohesion, making nice memories and creating bubbles of family life amidst the hectic everyday routine. This requires having special spaces for the whole family, and spaces for intimate togetherness in the case of a couple. A place where everyone gathers and feels utterly at home. Where everyone can have a good time together, whether it be playing games or having a cuddle, enjoying a movie night or some joint reading time, planning your next holiday or feasting on delicious treats you have cooked together. Whatever you like to do as a couple or with the whole family should be given its very own special feel-good place in your home.

Where exactly this feel-good place should be depends on what is to happen there. A large dining table or even a relaxed lounge area is generally good as a special space for more than one person. The dining table is perfect for get-togethers and discussions, celebratory dinners and creative sessions, and a couch set with comfortable armchairs provides the perfect setting for chilled family evenings, an exciting bout of movie-bingeing or some good old-fashioned cuddling and tickling. Dining tables and lounge areas are also potentially perfect special spaces for couples.

When you're creating a special space for a group, everyone's opinions are important. What are the needs and wishes of each individual housemate? Making a collective moodboard is not only fun, but also a great family activity, consolidating everyone's ideas and perfectly fitting them all together.

A dining table can extend as far as the space allows. There definitely needs to be enough room for all family members, as well as for any friends or relatives who may join in. Some fold-up chairs or stools can be added as necessary. In a nearby storage space you can keep games, craft materials and anything else that everyone enjoys doing as a group.

The cuddling corner naturally also needs to be spacious enough – a sofa or two, plus some cosy armchairs, as well as beanbags and floor cushions are the foundations for many happy hours together. Don't forget to add blankets – and perhaps someone would like to loll around on a thick carpet instead?

Left It's not just the younger family members who occasionally like to slouch on the floor. Carpet and thick pillows have an important job here. *Below left* Pale furniture and pastel-coloured objects create a happy mood in your favourite seating area. *Below right* A 'round table' is the perfect hub for good communication.

AGAIN & AGAIN

Rituals are important when living with others, so try to revive old ones or invent new ones. Friday is movie night; on Saturdays you assemble your own pizza; and Sunday is reserved for afternoon games or storytelling – regular events are a great way of bringing everyone together.

ONTO THE *Sofa*

Line Nevers Krabbenhøft
SOFACOMPANY

As the head of design at Sofacompany, the Danish upholstered furniture manufacturer, Line lets her creative ideas flow. She herself loves the classic style with a modern twist and makes her designs real eye-catchers. She designed her own home as a mix of 'old and new' in combination with 'not too excitable and extravagant'. For Line's designs and other inspirations, see sofacompany.com.

Left *Lots of cushions, flowers and a view of the greenery outside make your favourite sofa a wellbeing seat.*

Where is your favourite place in your home? And why is your special space right there?
I love most of all spending my time in our living room – or rather on the two sofas I designed myself. They form the centre of our family life and at the same time they are a retreat for self-care. The sofas face each other in the middle of the room and, with their soft curves, they form an exciting contrast to the clean, cool metal of the coffee table. In addition, there is a lounge chair in the room, made of leather and chrome, which functions at times as a sculpture, at times as a seat for guests. A large shelf along the wall holds novels as well as design books, coffee-table books and interior design magazines. A round, leather-framed mirror on the wall and an old kilim rug in harmonious rust and brown hues on the floor provide a pleasant ambience. In addition, I have arranged selected artful table lamps, various design objects and personal mementoes on the window sills, including the Eames Bird and some inspiring illustrated books.

And what exactly do you do in this space? Do you relax, come up with creative ideas . . . ?
Everything is possible here. Above all, I relax in my special space with a few magazines or a good book. I watch TV or spend time here with friends and guests. Sometimes I even work here – but that actually happens more in the study right next door.

In your opinion, which elements are a must in a special space? Comfortable furniture, woollen blankets and cushions, atmospheric lighting, a fantastic view . . . ?
A favourite corner needs harmony and a welcoming ambience. A deep sofa with soft cushions, snuggly textiles, shapely lamps and a few candles are perfect for an atmospheric light.

Left Light also plays an important role. The floor lamp creates a nice atmosphere.
Right This special space offers room for many dear friends, good conversations and delicious meals.

also visually fit into the room or, even better, into the entire home. Modular sofas are currently particularly popular due to their versatility and flexibility. So, if you like rearranging furniture, move house on a regular basis or if you have a child who is about to move out, the best thing to do is to opt for a modular sofa. Depending on requirements, modules can be added, removed or rearranged at any time. A modular sofa is also a good idea for those who don't currently have a lot of living space but want to upgrade and move to a larger home at some point. You start with two or three modules and add more later when there is more space or the family grows. Another trend is deep, low lounge sofas, as many people these days prefer to lie on the settee rather than sit on it.

What are good colours and materials for a special space?

Personally, I love the palette of natural colours because they create a tranquil, harmonious atmosphere. Others, on the other hand, are more comfortable, with brighter colours. When it comes to materials, a mix is always good. Hard and soft, cold and warm – these are contrasts that bring a certain vivacity.

Why does every home need a sofa?

Because the sofa is the heart of the home where the family comes together – to cuddle, to play and to laugh; for a home cinema evening with popcorn, to tell stories and to have good conversations; for togetherness, but also for me-time. After the bed, it is the softest and most comfortable piece of furniture in the entire home. Just like in your bed, you can simply take a nap in between activities or enjoy a particularly comfortable and tasty breakfast.

What makes a good sofa? What should you look out for when choosing?

The perfect sofa always suits the people who live on and with it. This means that it should have the size and properties needed. And of course it must

And what about armchairs?

Armchairs are a chapter in themselves. They can easily be integrated into any part of your home, because there is always space somewhere for this solitary piece of furniture. Personally, I like to put them into unexpected places, like the kitchen or the hallway. But of course they also perfectly complement a sofa corner.

"

My special space? A sofa in the living room!

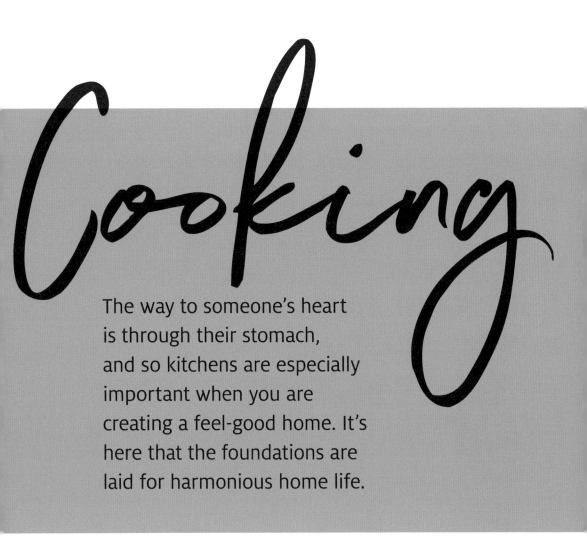

Cooking

The way to someone's heart is through their stomach, and so kitchens are especially important when you are creating a feel-good home. It's here that the foundations are laid for harmonious home life.

For most people, the kitchen is the centre of the home. It's where the day starts with a coffee or tea at an ungodly hour, where the most delicious dishes are prepared and where everyone comes together for meals. It's where children brood over homework at the table, and where hungry teenagers rummage through the refrigerator late at night. It's where, sometimes, there's only time to gobble down a quick sandwich, and where, other times, we feast, talk and laugh until late into the night. The most gripping discussions and the best parties happen in the kitchen, in the space between stove, larder and dining table.

Over time, the kitchen has gone from being purely functional to a place where much more happens than just meal preparation. That in itself is a good enough reason to give it the attention it deserves and to transform it into a feel-good place.

FOR 1001 *Flavours*

Aromatic fragrances and a beautifully laid table are enough to get anyone's mouth watering. It doesn't always have to be fine china – attractive earthenware can be just as good, if not better.

TONE IN TONE

While in the past the best crockery was only taken out of the cupboard for special occasions, things are much more relaxed today. Mix and match is the motto, with different colours and materials, old and new all combined into one relaxed ensemble.

Bottom far left and left Display your favourite crockery on open shelves – this way, it is decorative and quickly to hand.
Below Natural materials, such as wood, linen and cotton, work well on the table.
Right Let everything be uncomplicated. It's much more important that all your loved ones are together.

" Eat what makes you happy.

Heart of the
HOME

At the very latest once stomachs start growling, everyone's bound to be heading for the kitchen. Yet this space is not just about cooking and eating; it's also where we work, play, celebrate and argue, chat and study. It's the family's control centre, with timetables and invitations stuck on the fridge, and it's also the special space of passionate hobby cooks, food cupboards and utensils and appliances for every conceivable purpose. There are a few things you need to do to equip this heart of the home for all its tasks and, ultimately, turn it into a feel-good kitchen.

Firstly let's talk about layout. Is your kitchen just a small room, perhaps with a narrow corridor-like shape? Or a large space with enough room for a dining table with bench and chairs? Is the kitchen a separate room with a door you can close when frying fish and boiling cabbage? Or is it an open kitchen unit that transitions virtually seamlessly into the dining and, subsequently, living area? The shape and size of the space plays a fundamental role in the way it is fitted out with kitchen cupboards, appliances and work spaces.

A narrow layout, for example, does not allow room for a dining area or even an generously sized table. Cupboards are ideally fixed in one or two opposite rows along both walls. These rows may connect up with one another via cupboards situated on the shorter side of the room. If the layout provides more space, the kitchen can be L-shaped, with both cupboard units meeting at a right angle in one corner of the room. Not only does this look more spacious, it also makes for shorter distances to cover when you are working. Another way of achieving an L-shape is by completely covering one wall with cupboards and work spaces and having a short kitchen unit extend at right angles into the room. This is incidentally also a great way of creating a visual boundary between kitchen and dining area.

If you're lucky enough to have a large kitchen, you can run riot and create kitchen units in a U-shape – that is, have kitchen furniture along three walls. You also need adequate space if you want a kitchen island. This practical, free standing combination of work space and storage area maximises use of the area in the middle. Kitchen islands can contain a stove or sink. And, under

Left A kitchen doesn't have to be enormous – a small kitchenette can be visually just as appealing.

Far left Natural shades and materials ensure a relaxed atmosphere.
Left Smooth wooden fronts transform the kitchen into a homely space.
Bottom A room without too many frills helps you enjoy your food and the company.

the work space, there's naturally room for a dishwasher or an oven. Even if there's a seamless transition between the kitchen and the living area, a kitchen island makes for a great way of visually separating the two. Another advantage is that on the other side of the island there's space for stools and hungry onlookers, breakfasting children and guests wanting to help out a bit with peeling and chopping.

No matter how you arrange your furniture or how large your kitchen is, it's important to optimise the distances you walk between appliances and to ensure that nothing causes obstruction when you're on your way to the sink to drain a hot pan of pasta, or if you need to add another dash of cream to a saucepan that's bubbling away on the stove. In other words, the corners of the stove-fridge-sink triangle should be strategically positioned and not too far apart. This will make your kitchen activities much less stressful.

But it's not just about the kitchen layout, of course. Work spaces also play a key role when it comes to feel-good kitchens. The rule of thumb is that you can never have too large an area. Anyone who cooks or bakes frequently will know all about this. Pots, baking trays, mixing bowls and ingredients quickly pile up because, what with the milk frother, coffee machine, kettle and toaster, there's hardly any space left to temporarily put things. This is why it's practical

Left Kitchen cabinets on delicate feet appear airy, and the free standing legs also make cleaning easier.
Below You don't have to limit stone surfaces to the kitchen countertops – they also make good floor material.
Right If there's enough space, choose the longest possible table. That way it won't be too crowded at your next get-together with friends.

on the one hand to keep lots of utensils and appliances stowed away in cupboards and on the other hand to plan for work spaces that are as large as possible.

And storage space? The same rule applies here. The more storage space you have, the less stress you'll suffer in the kitchen. If you want to avoid having wall units so as to create an airier atmosphere, you could incorporate a kitchen island with hidden storage space. Installing cupboards all the way up to the ceiling is another way to optimise space usage in smaller kitchens. If they have no handles, they'll almost be invisible.

And what about the dining area? Again the same rule applies: the larger the table, the better. That way, friends and family can get together for spontaneous, quick and uncomplicated meals or for festive banquets. In addition, a large table provides room for games and work, or pursuing crafts. Long benches can seat more guests, though individual chairs are often more comfortable.

Left *You fancy something healthy to eat? A quiche is always a good option, and vegetables and wholegrain dough are packed with nutrients.*
Below *A thick wooden board is an attractive way to present delicious bites.*
Bottom *Muesli and granola give you an energy boost at the start of the day and can be refined to taste.*

BON APPETIT!

Looking for some new inspiration? Check out these food bloggers for feel-good recipes:

- loveandlemons.com
- melissahemsley.com
- hungryhealthyhappy.com
- marthastewart.com

Mood
FOOD

Appetising aromas waft from the pan, gentle bubbling indicates that something tasty is being cooked up, and there's a tantalising golden glint of a cheesy topping in the oven – any kitchen can become a feel-good kitchen if good food is being prepared. Conversely, if a kitchen features a stunning design and the dining area has been lovingly set up, then the food also needs to play its part in the overall experience.

Mmmmm, delicious! Comfort food is like a warm hug. Some dishes bring back fond childhood memories, tasting like mum's and granny's staples, while others remind us of amazing holidays, and delight our tastebuds. Some are a source of culinary solace, but every single one is just plain good – food of the soul.

What's most important is that you take your time. Take your time to prepare things – at ease on your own or together with family and friends. Take your time to set the table – with nice crockery, candles and flowers for a special meal or just with your favourite plate and a nice glass for a simple evening meal. Take your time to enjoy everything too – on your own, with your partner or with a large group of loved ones. Let every delicious bite melt in the mouth.

Quality ingredients are of course equally important. Buy regional and seasonal produce, opt for fresh foods rather than those that have been shrink-wrapped and clocked up many food miles. Not only is this better for the environment and the climate, it also means you'll be choosing products that give your body all the good stuff it needs at that moment. So it's better to go for strawberries picked fresh from the fields in early summer rather than at Christmas time, and enjoying cabbage and root vegetables in winter – simply seasonal food for body and soul.

Cooking
WITH
STYLE

Magdalena Höhn
Bulthaup

For the managing director of Bulthaup Köln GmbH, the kitchen is a very special place in the home. 'It's filled with smells and tastes, colours and shapes, technology and tools – and it has to be practical on the one hand, but also comfortable and presentable on the other.' Her own kitchen, by the way, is tidy and plain, with barely any appliances visible and plenty of worktop space. You can find ideas on bulthaup.com.

Left *Colourful cupboards without handles look so much more homely and less like a kitchen workspace.*

A kitchen as the central point of the home needs to be well thought out. How does kitchen planning work?

A high-quality kitchen is individually adapted to each user. That's what makes this job so exciting. The first step is getting to know each other. What are the client's needs, desires and living conditions? And vice versa, the customer also gets to know us and our style, and then decides whether it feels good. We accompany our customers over a long period of time, so we need to be able to trust each other. If everything fits, the next step is the practical needs analysis. What does the room look like? What does the floor look like? What light is there in the room? What system is used? What do the surfaces, handles and devices look like? What is the colour scheme? On this basis, we create an initial concept and a first cost estimation. This is followed by the elaboration of the details, the commissioning and finally the production and assembly.

What are the basic elements a kitchen absolutely must have?

In the kitchen you need the ability to wash, prepare and cook. The necessary appliances are therefore elementary – hob and oven, fridge-freezer and dishwasher. In addition, of course, a sink and plenty of workspace. The storage space should be optimally designed and offer room for food supplies on the one hand, and on the other also room for kitchen utensils, small appliances and so on. Numerous drawers and pull-out elements in the work area are very practical. The appropriate working height is also important – it can make sense to place one or the other appliance much higher up (the dishwasher makes more sense here than the oven). It would be nice to incorporate a sitting or standing area, no matter how small, for enjoying your morning coffee or tea. However, it is

What makes a kitchen feel homely?

It's all about a successful and balanced combination of different surfaces. Every surface needs its counterpart. If the floor features liquid screed, for example, wooden elements can bring the desired tension but also warmth into the room. Conversely, a room with lots of structure also needs smooth surfaces for a balanced ambience. It's always the interplay of various factors that gives us a comfortable feeling. Personal favourites also play an important role, such as the collection of selected cups, special knives or family portraits. The same applies to textiles, if only in the form of cloth napkins.

What is the best way to create a feel-good atmosphere?

You always have to look at the overall situation. Is it possible to integrate the kitchen furniture into the living space? Our furniture, for example, never looks 'kitcheny' and can also become an extension to the sideboard in the living room. It makes sense to hide apparatuses behind fronts and to use an integrated extractor fan system. Free standing elements can serve as a link between the kitchen and living areas, and can accommodate crockery on one side and books and plants on the other.

not absolutely necessary. The same also applies to devices such as a wine climate cabinet, a vacuuming drawer and so on. In short: a kitchen should be aesthetically and sensibly designed for the respective user and appear clear and logical in its layout. It should radiate security and durability, and be a nice, solid workspace that doesn't just appear like a showroom.

Which materials and colours are particularly appropriate for this?

The materials always have to be easy to care for, robust and yet aesthetically pleasing. Laminates, stainless steel and aluminium are particularly good choices, for example. Natural stone as well as artificial stone, that is, a material composite, make perfect sense for work surfaces. When it comes to colours, there is no right or wrong, just the question of what goes well with the room? Should the kitchen be visually restrained or would you prefer it to stand out and catch the eye? Customers often choose the colour white for their kitchen walls and cupboards because the food, the additional furniture and even the people themselves are the elements that bring the colours into the room. And ultimately the people play the starring role, of course.

A quality kitchen is a design object.

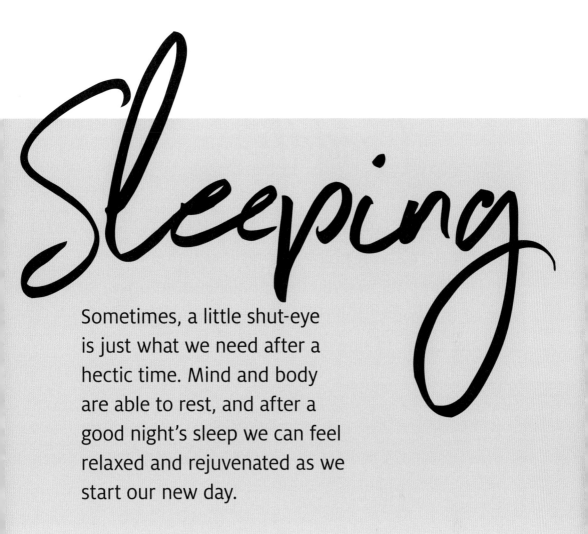

Sleeping

Sometimes, a little shut-eye is just what we need after a hectic time. Mind and body are able to rest, and after a good night's sleep we can feel relaxed and rejuvenated as we start our new day.

Humans spend around one-third of their lives in bed, and, if all goes well, they'll be using this time to sleep deeply, steadily and restfully – because sleep is fundamentally important. Whether the optimum time is six, eight or more hours varies from person to person. What is for sure, however, is that, without adequate sleep, mind and body cannot function well. When we're sleep-deprived, we're unable to concentrate, our reactions are impeded and we quickly become irritable. Over the long term, lack of sleep can even make us ill.

This is why it's all the more important for us to indulge in as much rest and sleep as we need. While counting sheep may not necessarily achieve the outcome we're looking for, a nicely furnished bedroom, a pleasant room temperature and a super-comfortable bed with matching mattress can.

COME *Cuddle*

Soft and fluffy, light but warm and toasty –
the best part about going to bed is the many
blankets and pillows you can finally cuddle up
with at the end of the day, feeling all snuggly
until the break of dawn.

INNER LIFE

When it comes to duvets, it's what's
inside that counts. Down keeps you
warm in winter and cool in summer.
Cotton is breathable and moisture-
regulating – ideal in summer. Kapok
is another natural fibre and very
light. Sheep's wool is a good moisture
absorber, camel hair evens out great
temperature differences, and synthetic
fibres are particularly easy to care for.

*Left Linen bed clothes are pleasantly
cool, especially in summer.*
*Top right If you shiver easily, an extra
blanket will always be welcome.*
*Centre right A large duvet for two?
Usually this only works if both parties
are quiet sleepers.*
*Bottom right You'd best check for
yourself which pillow shape and
thickness is the right one for you.*

> "You can never have too many pillows and blankets.

A good Night's SLEEP

During the night, phases of deep sleep alternate with phases of light sleep and REM. During the REM phases we dream intensively and our eyes move rapidly under their lids – hence the name Rapid Eye Movement. Your brain is awake during the whole time, using your sleep to tidy up and, if necessary, make repairs. It forms new connections, consolidates the things you've learned during the day and deletes anything that is not needed. It's not the brain alone, however, that benefits from night-time rest; the rest of your body does too. Your nerve cells regenerate. Your blood pressure drops during the phases of deep sleep. Your muscles relax and your digestive system winds down. Damaged cells are repaired and even your skin regenerates itself. Your mind has a chance to process the day's experiences, and in addition, your immune system makes good use of the rest phase to fight any viruses or bacteria in your body. So it's definitely worth making sure you get a good night's sleep.

Left *Covered in velvet, this bed sets the matching colour scheme for all the accompanying linens, bedspreads and throws.*

Sleep patterns alternate in the same way as day and night, and light and darkness play an essential role here. Yet the hormone melatonin is also heavily involved. It is formed in darkness, and one of its tasks is to encourage tiredness and sleep. Light, meanwhile, suppresses melatonin production. The body gets going again and the person comes awake.

Not all people need the same amount of sleep or get tired at the same time, of course. Between five or six and nine hours of sleep is considered normal, depending on individual needs. Our sleep requirements are influenced by various factors and may fluctuate. Genetics also play a role, as does the season, but working lives and stress levels also affect an individual's sleep requirements. This is why we should worry less about the number of sleeping hours and more about the ability to wake up in the morning, feeling rested and energised.

'Early birds' are awake particularly early and are also very productive in the morning, but find it difficult to stay awake late. 'Night owls', on the other hand, are active until late into the night but are likely to struggle to get out of bed early.

Whether or not you sleep well and restfully and feel energised to start the day is also determined by your

Right In this modern version of
the four-poster bed, the fabric
panels ensure even more calm.
Below You'll sleep well in
natural materials like
cotton, wool and linen.
Far right With a wall behind you,
you won't need a headboard.

bedroom, and this revolves around
the bed itself. A bed should be large
enough for you to properly stretch
out. For families, you can never have
too big a bed, because it's often not
just on Sunday mornings that kids
like to hop into their parents' bed and
rouse them before time. No, someone
will constantly wish to snuggle in
between mum and dad, perhaps after
having a bad dream or because their
own blankets and pillows were just
not comfortable enough. Whether
you go for a box-spring bed or a bed
with a slatted frame is a matter of
personal taste, as is the choice to have
a headboard or not, whether to have a
bed with drawers underneath or four
decorative legs, or whether you want
a bed canopy or storage space.

What plays an even greater role
than design when it comes to a good
night's sleep, however, is the mattress.
It lays the foundations for restful
sleep, which is why you need to read
up thoroughly and try lying on lots
of different models before deciding
on the one to buy. What's it going
to be? Latex, cold foam or classic
innerspring? Many factors are at play
when it comes to finding the right
mattress. Height, weight and body
shape, for example, are all particularly
important. Manufacturers classify the
firmness of their products into five
different degrees of hardness. The rule
of thumb is the heavier the person, the
firmer the mattress. What's important
is that the spine forms a straight line
when you are sleeping on your side.

Far left Walls in dark grey-blue and furniture made of natural wood make the room an inviting oasis of calm.
Left Indoor plants are air fresheners and also a pretty privacy screen.
Bottom White walls and white ceilings, plus light floors – this is how a bedroom may radiate friendliness and serenity. Even the desk in front of the window doesn't disturb the ambience.

A proper slatted frame will support the mattress, not only ensuring good ventilation from underneath, but greater comfort too.

The right climate conditions in the bedroom will also make for a good, comfortable night's sleep. While the living areas we spend our day in can be kept a little warmer, we sleep better at lower temperatures of around 18°C (64°F). Regular bursts of intense aeration will ensure that the used air is always replaced with fresh oxygen. And here's a little decorative hack: plants produce oxygen and, in the case of some species, also purify the air of pollutants, making for perfect indoor climate conditions (see page 159 for more detail on this).

Light and sun invigorate the body and get it moving. So, in the bedroom, darkness is best for ensuring a good night's rest. The light from street lanterns or illuminated shop windows right in front of the window can be blocked out by thick, lined curtains or blackout blinds.

Left *Even if you don't want a bedside table, you need at least a shelf for reading glasses, an alarm clock and the like.*
Below *The reading lights can of course also hang from the ceiling, as long as you can switch them on from the bed.*
Right *In summer, simple sheets will suffice if a thick blanket is too warm.*

FIRM SUPPORT

A good pillow supports your head and relieves your spine. As with duvets, a wide variety of fillings is available for you to choose from, ranging from spelt to down. If you are prone to tension aches, you may sleep particularly well with a moulded orthopaedic pillow.

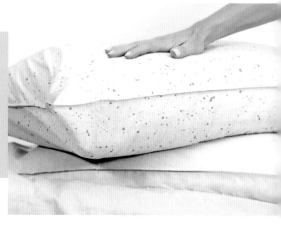

SLEEP
Well

For many people, just getting to sleep is difficult enough. To avoid endless tossing and turning in frustration, it's best to only go to bed when you're really tired. This will significantly increase your chances of falling asleep quickly. Still got unfinished business from the day spinning around in your head? Rituals can help slow the stream of thoughts. Meditation or a calming tea are both good options here. Conversely, smartphones and similar devices should be avoided – not only because of the bright light emitted from their screens but also because they are a source of temptation to keep scrolling. Constantly looking at the clock is another no-no; it will only increase the pressure of needing to fall asleep.

If you really are finding it hard to drift off, you're better off heading to the living room to read a good book or listen to restful music rather than tossing

GETTING HELP

Sleeping pills are not a permanent solution. Any medication should only be used for a short period of time, especially when administered without medical advice. If you have a chronic sleep problems, it is better to see a professional. Sleep medicine experts, or sophrologists, specialise in this area and can help you recover from deprivation.

and turning in bed. Only return to the sack when you're truly tired. Heavy evening meals keep the digestive tract active overnight and prevent you from sleeping, and smoking before bed is similarly counterproductive. Some people are more sensitive than others to caffeine – they are advised to limit coffee and black tea consumption to the first half of the day. Alcohol consumption can also affect sleep.

Getting adequate exercise, on the other hand, will have a positive impact on sleep, as long as it is done during the day and not right before bed. Just a walk in the fresh air will suffice to make you feel tired at night.

If you are spending a lot of time in bed but not sleeping much, shorten this time. Simply go to bed later and get up earlier.

Good NIGHT

Holly Becker
decor8

Holly is an interior designer and trend expert. In 2006 she founded her blog decor8 to share the latest and most beautiful interior trends and to present fabulous homes and creative people. And that's not the only thing – Holly is also a stylist, photographer, writer and presenter, and teaches online courses on her favourite topics of interior design, social media and photography. More on decor8blog.com and Instagram @decor8

What do you love most about interior design and design in general?
Using colours, fabrics, furniture and accessories, people can create the exact style of the interior design that best suits their lifestyle. Home is the one place in the world where we can truly be ourselves and do the things we love most. With our furnishings, we create a stage for our lives in a way that suits our personality. I'm very intuitive and creative, so decorating and beautifying a space is an emotional and deeply thoughtful process for me. It's like a blank canvas on which I can express myself and my creativity. Furnishing is so much more than just putting objects in the right place.

And which of your many activities or tasks do you enjoy the most?
Oh, I love them all – attending creative events and trade fairs, researching new trends, advising, writing, developing and styling interior concepts. All these things are united under one umbrella, so to speak, and that is interior design, my great passion. So I'm looking for and developing projects that fit under that overall umbrella. My work makes me happy and gives me a lot of energy.

In your opinion, what items of furniture does a bedroom need?
This room is intended for your relaxation, for you to rest, and for good nights full of restful sleep. Therefore, the most important piece of furniture is a high-quality bed. I can't possibly stress that enough. It will probably cost you a tidy sum of money, but it's actually the very best investment you can make; after all, you're investing in your own sleep. Anything you can organise, arrange and decorate in the bedroom to ensure peaceful nights is therefore a good idea.

Left The pale sage green of the walls brings nature from outside into the bedroom.

Left Soft hues help body and mind to wind down at the end of the day.
Right Cotton, wood, ceramics – natural materials look good, and also make you feel good.

feel relaxed. This routine helps me to wind down, perhaps after a stressful day, and I'm sure to sleep the sleep of angels.

Which colours are best suited to this room?

The colours you like best. In my bedroom, they are light, natural tones – cream, a light salmon pink and a soft peach hue. If you prefer more intense colours, you should use these strong shades in such a way that they are behind you so that you do not look at a bright red or orange when you are falling asleep or waking up.

And what has no place in the bedroom?

Lots of stuff. Open shelves full of books and other favourite pieces are nice, but they add clutter to the bedroom. I would instead hide everything behind closed cupboard doors and in drawers. That way you don't have to lie in bed and look at all this visual noise. A bedroom needs to be tidy and visually calm for a great night's sleep – every single night. Large numbers of photos and art on the wall would also disturb this calm. You don't need them in this room. If you manage to reduce this visual unrest, you will gain a relaxed, safe place that feels good. In beautiful hotels and spas, the rooms are also kept very minimalistic and understated. This keeps your head clear and your thoughts calm.

How do you create a soothing atmosphere in this 'quiet' room?

One excellent way to create a relaxing, soothing ambience is to use scented oils. I always put a few drops into the water of my aroma diffuser and it soon smells simply wonderful. Also, I have a good Bluetooth speaker so I can play some relaxing music. Plus I light an atmospheric candle, and before I go to bed, I do some yoga exercises in the bedroom. This helps me to switch off completely, and so I can make sure that everything feels good when I go to bed. There is a lovely scent in the room, I've done yoga and

And what about the materials?

Natural materials are the best in the bedroom. Cotton and linen for the bedding and a wool rug on the floor. These materials are not only durable, they are also breathable and have a positive effect on the indoor climate. I make sure that non-toxic paints, floors and so on are used in our home.

What does the bedroom of your personal dreams look like?

Oh, I'm dreaming of an en suite bathroom with a large bathtub. There would also be a large walk-in cupboard for my clothes. Plus, of course, a stunning view from the window of the nature outside, of trees and meadows. That would be simply awesome.

A good, restful sleep – that is the goal.

" Home is not
a place,
it's an emotion.

MANUFACTURERS AND FAVOURITE SHOPS

Bathroom
bathstore.com
designerbathroomstore.co.uk
fink.store
frigbath.com
traditional-bathrooms.com
vipp.dk

Carpets & Floors
benuta.de
dinesen.com
flooranddecor.com
heavenrugs.com
parador.de
rugs-direct.com

Furniture & Furnishings
boconcept.de
bolia.com
carlhansen.com
formandrefine.com
fritzhansen.com
gubi.dk
montana.dk
raumplus.de
sofacompanyprofessional.com
stringfurniture.com
thonet.de
tolix.fr
vitra.com

Home Accessories
bloomingville.com
bylassen.com
danishcollection.co.uk
designhousestockholm.com
fermliving.com
hay.dk
housedoctor.dk
hubsch-interior.com
iblaursen.dk
lenebjerre.com
madamstoltz.dk
normann-copenhagen.com
sostrenegrene.com
tinekhome.com

Lighting
andtradition.com
artemide.com
flos.com
hkliving.nl
lightyears.dk
louispoulsen.com
lumens.com
muuto.com
northern.no
tomdixon.net

Kitchen, Crockery etc.
bulthaup.com/en/
dottirnordicdesign.com
eggersmann.com
everythingkitchens.com
nicolasvahe.com
reformcph.com
rosendahl.com
siematic.com
stelton.com
thekitchencompany.co.uk
usakitchens.com

Textiles
beddinghouse.com
bynord.com
designersguild.com
fischbacher.com
hessnatur.com
himla.com
lexingtoncompany.com

Wallpaper & Paints
borastapeter.se
cole-and-son.com
eijffinger.com
farrow-ball.com
littlegreene.de
photowall.de
sandbergwallpaper.com
wearewallhaus.com

A selection of our favourite online shops:

ambientedirect.com
anthropologie.com
boheme-living.com
chairish.com
connox.de
crateandbarrel.com
dykeanddean.com
finnishdesignshop.com
grandinroad.com
habitat.co.uk
hema.com
homeplace.eu
jotex.de
juniqe.de
macys.com
merci-merci.com
nordicelements.co.uk
nordicnest.de
nunido.de
papustories.com
room356.co.uk
schoolhouse.com
skandihome.com
smallable.com
target.com
thelittlehouseshop.co.uk
thewhitecompany.com
tikamoon.de
trouva.com
urbanara.de
urbanoutfitters.com
wayfair.com
zocohome.com

About us

Marion Hellweg

. . . is the editor-in-chief of the lifestyle magazine *Living & More* and manages the Nord Liv editorial office as an interiors and lifestyle journalist. Marion also works as a stylist and interior designer and has established herself as a successful author and influencer. Her lifestyle books *Tiny Homes, The Green Life, Pure & Simple: Mindful Living* and *Living with Natural Materials* were published by Prestel. She lives in Munich with her daughter Florentine.

You can also see and hear more about her on Instagram: @marionhellweg

Frederike Treu

. . . lives in Worpswede near Bremen with her sons, husband and pets. A cultural scientist, Frederike became self-employed in 2009 after holding various positions in publishing houses and agencies. Since then, she has mainly written about her two great passions: lifestyle and gardening. Her articles are regularly published in various interior and lifestyle magazines, among others, for which she writes reports, portraits and regular columns. She is also the author of several books.

Thanks

A big thank you goes to Frederike – this book would not have been possible without your strong writing skills! I would also like to thank all the photographers, photo agencies, manufacturers and companies who have made their beautiful images available to us for this book. I would also like to thank Florentine and my family and friends for their love and support. Last but not least, a warm 'Merci!' to the entire Prestel team for their wonderful cooperation. I would particularly like to thank Julie Kiefer for her confidence and commitment as well as Sabine Loos for her wonderful layout – a creative collaboration couldn't look any better.

PICTURE CREDITS

p.3: Emma Groenenboom/CocoFeature; p.4: Vossberg; p.5: Sarah Domandl/Saripicture; p.7: Emma Groenenboom/CocoFeature, Krista Keltanen/Living Inside, Hans Mossel; p.8: Malcom Menzies/Living Inside; p.11: Emma Groenenboom/CocoFeature, Tina Witherspoon; p.12: Unsplash, Marshall; p.14: Sofa Stories, Søstrene Grene; p.16: Unsplash; p.18 Sylwia Gervais, Unsplash; p.20: The Bunker; p.23: Unsplash, Dinesen, Juan Baraja/Abaton; p.24: David Watson Architect; pp.26–7: Laura Schiebel, estudio lak, Daniela Mac Adden/surpressagency; pp.28–7: Anne den Haan/CocoFeature, Greg Cox/Bureaux; p.30: Margriet Hoekstra/CocoFeatures, Bodil Johansson, Krista Keltanen/Living Inside; p.33: My Homestyle, Warren Heath/Bureaux; pp.34–7: Haus Gables/Naaro; p.38: Unsplash; p.40: Marrakech Tiles; p.41: House Doctor, Dinesen, Anitta Behrendt/Living Inside; p.42: Hans Mossel; p.45: In2Architecture; p.47: Søstrene Grene, In2Architecture; p.48: Hans Mossel; p.49: Raumplus; p.50: Hübsch Interior; p.51: Sweet Living; p.52: Peter Kragballe; pp.54–5: Mural, Liv Interior, Fischbacher; p.56: Hans Mossel; s. 58: Schöner Wohnen; p.59: Bungalow, Pernille Kaalund/House of Pictures; p.60: photowall; p.61: Mural; p.62: Norsu; p.63: Pernille Kaalund/House of Pictures, Pernille Folcarelli; pp.64–66: Dulux; p.68: Peter Kragballe; p.69: Koloart, Julia Berlin; p.70: Kolorat; p.71: Peter Kragballe; p.72: Liv Interior: pp.74–5: Søstrene Grene, Hans Mossel; p.76: Søstrene Grene; p.78: Søstrene Grene; p.79: Unsplash; p.80: Søstrene Grene; p.81: Broste Copenhagen, Anitta Behrendt/Livinginside; p.83: Unsplash; p.84: Margriet Hoekstra/CocoFeatures; p.85: Michael Weniger; pp.86–7: Søstrene Grene; p.88: Hans Mossel; pp.90–92: String, Schlaraffia, House Doctor; p.92: Ideal Home; p.94: Car Möbel, Bloomingville; p.95: Sweet Living; p.96: Ideal Home; p.97: Int2Architecture; p.99: Muuto, Lundqvist, Lockwood; p.100: Gitte Staerbo; p.101: Lilly Koslowsky; pp.102–3: Ideal Home; p.104: Liv Interior; pp.106–107: Liv Interior, Eagle Products, Affari; p.108: Liv Interior; p.110: Liv Interior; p.111: Carl Hansen; p.112: Rubelli; p.113: Broste Copenhagen; p.115: by Lassen, Vitra, p.116: Carl Hansen, Form & Refine; p.118: Liv Interior; p.119: Form & Refine; p.120 House Doctor; p.121: Form & Refine; p.122: Urban Outfitters; pp.124–5: Stocubo, Marshall, Bang & Olufsen, Raumfeld; p.126: WoodUpp; pp.128–9: WoodUpp, Zilenzio; p.130: House Doctor, Marrakech Tiles; p.131: Madam Stoltz; p.132: Urban Outfitters; p.133: Sarah Domandl/Saripicture; p.134: Marion Hellweg; p.135: String; p.136: House Doctor; pp.138–9: Lampenwelt; p.140: House Doctor; p.142: Int2Architecture; p.143: Krista Keltanen/Living Inside; p.144: Emma Groenenboom/CocoFeature; p.145: Int2Architecture; p.146: Vossberg; p.148: Int2Architecture, The Bunker; p.150: Artemide; p.151: Artemide; p.152: Artemide; p.153: Dinesen; p.154: Ikea; pp.156–7: Unsplash, Hübsch Interior, Broste Copenhagen; p.158: House Doctor; p.160: Ideal Home; p.161: Bloomingville; p.162: Ideal Home; p.163: Blogspot; p.164: Ib Laursen; Unsplash; p.166: Bloomingville; p.167: Jules Villbrandt; pp.168–169: Sweet Living; p.170: Hans Mossel: pp.172–3: Hans Mossel, Sofa Company, Karup; p.174: Johanna Hagbard; p.176: Hans Mossel; p.177: Ideal Home; p.178: Bloomingville, Ideal Home, Krista Keltanen/Living Inside; p.181: Ideal Home, Vitra; p.182: Margriet Hoekstra/CocoFeatures; p.183: Sofa Company; p.184: Jonah Samyn/CocoFeatures; p.185: Pernille Kaalund/House of Pictures; p.186: Granit; pp.188–9: Unsplash, Broste Copenhagen, Bungalow, de Buyer; p.190: Int2Architecture; p.192: Søstrene Grene; p.193: Jonah Samyn/CocoFeatures, Søstrene Grene; p.194: Vipp, Ideal Home; p.195: Anitta Behrendt/Livinginside; pp.196–7: Unsplash, Lisa Bjorner/Living Inside; p.198: Sabine Burkunk; pp.200–201: Bulthaup; p.202: Novamobile; pp.204–5: Textilwerk, Søstrene Grene, by Skagen, Alva; p.206: Little Grene; p.208: Himla, Ideal Home; p.209: ferm Living; p.210: Schöner Wohnen; p.211: Lexington, Marimekko; p.212: Int2Architecture, Alva; p.213: Schlaraffia; p.214: Pernille Kaalund/House of Pictures; p.215: Anoushka Rokebrand; p.216: Jonah Samyn/CocoFeatures; p.217: Södahl; pp.218–19: Malcom Menzies/Living Inside; p.220: Holly Marder: p.222: Portrait Marion Hellweg: Sarah Domandl/Saripicture, Portrait Frederike Treu: Ingo Jagels

© Prestel Verlag, Munich · London · New York, 2023
A member of the Penguin Random House Verlagsgruppe GmbH
Neumarkter Strasse 28
81673 Munich

Library of Congress Control Number is available; a CIP catalogue record for this book is available from the British Library.

Idea and concept: Marion Hellweg, marionhellweg.com
Text: Frederike Treu
Editorial direction: Julie Kiefer
Project management, translation and typesetting: Sylvia Goulding, Les Arques
Copyeditor: Mike Goulding
Proofreader: Diana Vowles
Design and layout: Sabine Loos, Berlin
Cover image: Anitta Behrendt/ Living Inside
Back cover images: Johanna Hagbard, Int2architecture, Schöner Wohnen
Production management: Cilly Klotz
Separations: Schnieber Graphik GmbH, Munich
Printing and binding: Livonia Print, Riga

Penguin Random House Verlagsgruppe
FSC® N001967

Printed in Latvia

ISBN 978-3-7913-8937-0

www.prestel.com